HBR'S
10
MUST
READS

For
New
Managers

HBR's 10 Must Reads series is the definitive collection of ideas and best practices for aspiring and experienced leaders alike. These books offer essential reading selected from the pages of *Harvard Business Review* on topics critical to the success of every manager.

Titles include:

HBR's 10 Must Reads 2015
HBR's 10 Must Reads 2016
HBR's 10 Must Reads 2017
HBR's 10 Must Reads on Change Management
HBR's 10 Must Reads on Collaboration
HBR's 10 Must Reads on Communication
HBR's 10 Must Reads on Emotional Intelligence
HBR's 10 Must Reads on Innovation
HBR's 10 Must Reads on Leadership
HBR's 10 Must Reads on Making Smart Decisions
HBR's 10 Must Reads on Managing Across Cultures
HBR's 10 Must Reads on Managing People
HBR's 10 Must Reads on Managing Yourself
HBR's 10 Must Reads on Strategic Marketing
HBR's 10 Must Reads on Strategy
HBR's 10 Must Reads on Teams
HBR's 10 Must Reads: The Essentials

For
New
Managers

HARVARD BUSINESS REVIEW PRESS
Boston, Massachusetts

Names: Container of (work): Hill, Linda A. (Linda Annette), 1956- Becoming the boss. | Harvard Business Review Press, issuing body.
Title: HBR's 10 must reads for new managers.
Other titles: HBR's ten must reads for new managers | Harvard Business Review's 10 must reads for new managers | HBR's 10 must reads (Series)
Description: Boston, Massachusetts : Harvard Business Review Press, [2017] | Series: HBR's 10 must reads
Identifiers: LCCN 2016040077 | ISBN 9781633693029 (pbk.)
Subjects: LCSH: Management. | Leadership.
Classification: LCC HD31.2 .H37 2017 | DDC 658—dc23 LC record available at https://lccn.loc.gov/201604007

ISBN: 978-1-63369-302-9
eISBN: 978-1-63369-303-6

Contents

Becoming the Boss   1
by Linda A. Hill

Leading the Team You Inherit   19
by Michael D. Watkins

Saving Your Rookie Managers from Themselves   35
by Carol A. Walker

Managing the High-Intensity Workplace   49
by Erin Reid and Lakshmi Ramarajan

Harnessing the Science of Persuasion   61
by Robert B. Cialdini

What Makes a Leader?   79
by Daniel Goleman

The Authenticity Paradox   101
by Herminia Ibarra

Managing Your Boss   115
by John J. Gabarro and John P. Kotter

How Leaders Create and Use Networks   133
by Herminia Ibarra and Mark Lee Hunter

Management Time: Who's Got the Monkey?   151
by William Oncken, Jr., and Donald L. Wass

BONUS ARTICLE
How Managers Become Leaders   165
by Michael D. Watkins

About the Contributors   181
Index   183

**HBR'S
10
MUST
READS**

For
New
Managers

Becoming the Boss

by Linda A. Hill

EVEN FOR THE MOST GIFTED individuals, the process of becoming a leader is an arduous, albeit rewarding, journey of continuous learning and self-development. The initial test along the path is so fundamental that we often overlook it: becoming a boss for the first time. That's a shame, because the trials involved in this rite of passage have serious consequences for both the individual and the organization.

Executives are shaped irrevocably by their first management positions. Decades later, they recall those first months as transformational experiences that forged their leadership philosophies and styles in ways that may continue to haunt and hobble them throughout their careers. Organizations suffer considerable human and financial costs when a person who has been promoted because of strong individual performance and qualifications fails to adjust successfully to management responsibilities.

The failures aren't surprising, given the difficulty of the transition. Ask any new manager about the early days of being a boss—indeed, ask any senior executive to recall how he or she felt as a new manager. If you get an honest answer, you'll hear a tale of disorientation and, for some, overwhelming confusion. The new role didn't feel anything like it was supposed to. It felt too big for any one person to handle. And whatever its scope, it sure didn't seem to have anything to do with leadership.

In the words of one new branch manager at a securities firm: "Do you know how hard it is to be the boss when you are so out of control? It's hard to verbalize. It's the feeling you get when you have a child. On day X minus 1, you still don't have a child. On day X, all of a sudden you're a mother or a father and you're supposed to know everything there is to know about taking care of a kid."

Given the significance and difficulty of this first leadership test, it's surprising how little attention has been paid to the experiences of new managers and the challenges they face. The shelves are lined with books describing effective and successful leaders. But very few address the challenges of learning to lead, especially for the first-time manager.

For the past 15 years or so, I've studied people making major career transitions to management, focusing in particular on the star performer who is promoted to manager. My original ambition was to provide a forum for new managers to speak in their own words about what it means to learn to manage. I initially followed 19 new managers over the course of their first year in an effort to get a rare glimpse into their subjective experience: What did they find most difficult? What did they need to learn? How did they go about learning it? What resources did they rely upon to ease the transition and master their new assignments?

Since my original research, which I described in the first edition of *Becoming a Manager*, published in 1992, I've continued to study the personal transformation involved when someone becomes a boss. I've written case studies about new managers in a variety of functions and industries and have designed and led new-manager leadership programs for companies and not-for-profit organizations. As firms have become leaner and more dynamic—with different units working together to offer integrated products and services and with companies working with suppliers, customers, and competitors in an array of strategic alliances—new managers have described a transition that gets harder all the time.

Let me emphasize that the struggles these new managers face represent the norm, not the exception. These aren't impaired managers operating in dysfunctional organizations. They're ordinary people facing ordinary adjustment problems. The vast majority of them survive the transition and learn to function in their new role.

Idea in Brief

Ask new managers about their early days as bosses, and you'll hear tales of disorientation, even despair. As Hill points out, most novice bosses don't realize how sharply management differs from individual work. Hampered by misconceptions, they fail the trials involved in this rite of passage. And when they stumble, they jeopardize their careers and inflict staggering costs on their organizations.

How to avoid this scenario? Beware of common misconceptions about management: For example, subordinates don't necessarily obey your orders, despite your formal authority over them. You won't have more freedom to make things happen—instead, you'll feel constrained by organizational interdependencies. And you're responsible not only for maintaining your own operations—but also for initiating positive changes both inside and outside of your areas of responsibility.

Armed with *realistic* expectations, you'll be more likely to survive the transition to management—and generate valuable results for your organization.

But imagine how much more effective they would be if the transition were less traumatic.

To help new managers pass this first leadership test, we need to help them understand the essential nature of their role—what it truly means to be in charge. Most see themselves as managers and leaders; they use the rhetoric of leadership; they certainly feel the burdens of leadership. But they just don't get it.

Why Learning to Manage Is So Hard

One of the first things new managers discover is that their role, by definition a stretch assignment, is even more demanding than they'd anticipated. They are surprised to learn that the skills and methods required for success as an individual contributor and those required for success as a manager are starkly different—and that there is a gap between their current capabilities and the requirements of the new position.

In their prior jobs, success depended primarily on their personal expertise and actions. As managers, they are responsible for setting

Idea in Practice

To succeed as a new manager, Hill suggests *replacing myths with realities.*

Myth	Reality	To manage effectively . . .	Example
Managers wield significant authority and freedom to make things happen.	You are enmeshed in a web of relationships with people who make relentless and conflicting demands on you.	Build relationships with people outside your group that your team depends on to do its work.	A U.S. media-company manager charged with setting up a new venture in Asia initiated regular meetings on regional strategy between executives from both businesses.
Managers' power derives from their formal position in the company.	Your power comes from your ability to establish credibility with employees, peers, and superiors.	Demonstrate character (intending to do the right thing), managerial competence (listening more than talking), and influence (getting others to do the right thing).	An investment bank manager won employees' respect by shifting from showing off his technical competence to asking them about their knowledge and ideas.
Managers must control their direct reports.	Control doesn't equal commitment. And employees don't necessarily always follow orders.	Build commitment by empowering employees to achieve the team's goals—not ordering them.	Instead of demanding that people do things her way, a media manager insisted on clarity about team goals and accountability for agreed-upon objectives.

and implementing an agenda for a whole group, something for which their careers as individual performers haven't prepared them.

Take the case of Michael Jones, the new securities-firm branch manager I just mentioned. (The identities of individuals cited in this article have been disguised.) Michael had been a broker for 13 years and was a stellar producer, one of the most aggressive and innovative professionals in his region. At his company, new branch managers were generally promoted from the ranks on the basis of

Myth	Reality	To manage effectively . . .	Example
Managers lead their team by building relationships with individual members of the team.	Actions directed at one subordinate often negatively affect your other employees' morale or performance.	Pay attention to your team's overall performance. Use group-based forums for problem solving and diagnosis. Treat subordinates in an equitable manner.	After granting a special parking spot to a veteran salesman—a move that ruffled other salespeople's feathers—a new sales manager began leading his entire team rather than trying to get along well with each individual.

Don't Go It Alone

- Recognize that your boss is likely more tolerant of your questions and mistakes than you might expect

- Help your boss develop you. Instead of asking your boss to solve your problems, present ideas for how you

would handle a thorny situation, and solicit his thoughts on your ideas

- Find politically safe sources of coaching and mentoring from peers outside your function or in another organization

individual competence and achievements, so no one was surprised when the regional director asked him to consider a management career. Michael was confident he understood what it took to be an effective manager. In fact, on numerous occasions he had commented that if he had been in charge, he would have been willing and able to fix things and make life better in the branch. After a month in his new role, however, he was feeling moments of intense panic; it was harder than he had imagined to get his ideas implemented.

He realized he had given up his "security blanket" and there was no turning back.

Michael's reaction, although a shock to him, isn't unusual. Learning to lead is a process of learning by doing. It can't be taught in a classroom. It is a craft primarily acquired through on-the-job experiences—especially adverse experiences in which the new manager, working beyond his current capabilities, proceeds by trial and error. Most star individual performers haven't made many mistakes, so this is new for them. Furthermore, few managers are aware, in the stressful, mistake-making moments, that they are learning. The learning occurs incrementally and gradually.

As this process slowly progresses—as the new manager unlearns a mind-set and habits that have served him over a highly successful early career—a new professional identity emerges. He internalizes new ways of thinking and being and discovers new ways of measuring success and deriving satisfaction from work. Not surprisingly, this kind of psychological adjustment is taxing. As one new manager notes, "I never knew a promotion could be so painful."

Painful—and stressful. New managers inevitably ponder two questions: "Will I like management?" and "Will I be good at management?" Of course, there are no immediate answers; they come only with experience. And these two questions are often accompanied by an even more unsettling one: "Who am I becoming?"

A New Manager's Misconceptions

Becoming a boss is difficult, but I don't want to paint an unrelentingly bleak picture. What I have found in my research is that the transition is often harder than it need be because of new managers' misconceptions about their role. Their ideas about what it means to be a manager hold some truth. But, because these notions are simplistic and incomplete, they create false expectations that individuals struggle to reconcile with the reality of managerial life. By acknowledging the following misconceptions—some of which rise almost to the level of myth in their near-universal acceptance—new managers have a far greater chance of success. (For a comparison of

Why New Managers Don't Get It

BEGINNING MANAGERS OFTEN FAIL IN THEIR NEW ROLE, at least initially, because they come to it with misconceptions or myths about what it means to be a boss. These myths, because they are simplistic and incomplete, lead new managers to neglect key leadership responsibilities.

	Myth	Reality
Defining characteristic of the new role	Authority "Now I will have the freedom to implement my ideas."	Interdependency "It's humbling that someone who works for me could get me fired."
Source of power	Formal authority "I will finally be on top of the ladder."	"Everything but" "Folks were wary, and you really had to earn it."
Desired outcome	Control "I must get compliance from my subordinates."	Commitment "Compliance does not equal commitment."
Managerial focus	Managing one-on-one "My role is to build relationships with individual subordinates."	Leading the team "I need to create a culture that will allow the group to fulfill its potential."
Key challenge	Keeping the operation in working order "My job is to make sure the operation runs smoothly."	Making changes that will make the team perform better "I am responsible for initiating changes to enhance the group's performance."

the misconceptions and the reality, see the sidebar "Why New Managers Don't Get It.")

Managers wield significant authority

When asked to describe their role, new managers typically focus on the rights and privileges that come with being the boss. They assume the position will give them more authority and, with that, more freedom and autonomy to do what they think is best for the organization. No longer, in the words of one, will they be "burdened by the unreasonable demands of others."

New managers nursing this assumption face a rude awakening. Instead of gaining new authority, those I have studied describe finding themselves hemmed in by interdependencies. Instead of feeling free, they feel constrained, especially if they were accustomed to the relative independence of a star performer. They are enmeshed in a web of relationships—not only with subordinates but also with bosses, peers, and others inside and outside the organization, all of whom make relentless and often conflicting demands on them. The resulting daily routine is pressured, hectic, and fragmented.

"The fact is that you really are not in control of anything," says one new manager. "The only time I am in control is when I shut my door, and then I feel I am not doing the job I'm supposed to be doing, which is being with the people." Another new manager observes: "It's humbling that someone who works for me could get me fired."

The people most likely to make a new manager's life miserable are those who don't fall under her formal authority: outside suppliers, for example, or managers in another division. Sally McDonald, a rising star at a chemical company, stepped into a product development position with high hopes, impeccable credentials as an individual performer, a deep appreciation for the company's culture—and even the supposed wisdom gained in a leadership development course. Three weeks later, she observed grimly: "Becoming a manager is not about becoming a boss. It's about becoming a hostage. There are many terrorists in this organization that want to kidnap me."

Until they give up the myth of authority for the reality of negotiating interdependencies, new managers will not be able to lead effectively. As we have seen, this goes beyond managing the team of direct reports and requires managing the context within which the team operates. Unless they identify and build effective relationships with the key people the team depends upon, the team will lack the resources necessary to do its job.

Even if new managers appreciate the importance of these relationships, they often ignore or neglect them and focus instead on what seems like the more immediate task of leading those closest to them: their subordinates. When they finally do accept their network-builder role, they often feel overwhelmed by its demands.

Besides, negotiating with these other parties from a position of relative weakness—for that's often the plight of new managers at the
bottom of the hierarchy—gets tiresome.

But the dividends of managing the interdependencies are great.
While working in business development at a large U.S. media concern, Winona Finch developed a business plan for launching a Latin
American edition of the company's U.S. teen magazine. When the
project got tentative approval, Finch asked to manage it. She and
her team faced a number of obstacles. International projects were
not favored by top management, and before getting final funding,
Finch would need to secure agreements with regional distributors
representing 20% of the Latin American market—not an easy task
for an untested publication competing for scarce newsstand space.
To control costs, her venture would have to rely on the sales staff
of the Spanish-language edition of the company's flagship women's
magazine, people who were used to selling a very different kind of
product.

Winona had served a stint as an acting manager two years before,
so despite the morass of detail she had to deal with in setting up the
new venture, she understood the importance of devoting time and
attention to managing relationships with her superiors and peers.
For example, she compiled biweekly executive notes from her department heads that she circulated to executives at headquarters. To
enhance communication with the women's magazine, she initiated
regular Latin American board meetings at which top worldwide executives from both the teen and women's publications could discuss
regional strategy.

Her prior experience notwithstanding, she faced the typical
stresses of a new manager: "It's like you are in final exams 365 days a
year," she says. Still, the new edition was launched on schedule and
exceeded its business plan forecasts.

Authority flows from the manager's position

Don't get me wrong: Despite the interdependencies that con-
strain them, new managers do wield some power. The problem is
that most of them mistakenly believe their power is based on the

9

formal authority that comes with their now lofty—well, relatively speaking—position in the hierarchy. This operating assumption leads many to adopt a hands-on, autocratic approach, not because they are eager to exercise their new power over people but because they believe it is the most effective way to produce results.

New managers soon learn, however, that when direct reports are told to do something, they don't necessarily respond. In fact, the more talented the subordinate, the less likely she is to simply follow orders. (Some new managers, when pressed, admit that they didn't always listen to their bosses either.)

After a few painful experiences, new managers come to the unsettling realization that the source of their power is, according to one, "everything but" formal authority. That is, authority emerges only as the manager establishes credibility with subordinates, peers, and superiors. "It took me three months to realize I had no effect on many of my people," recalls one manager I followed. "It was like I was talking to myself."

Many new managers are surprised by how difficult it is to earn people's respect and trust. They are shocked, and even insulted, that their expertise and track record don't speak for themselves. My research shows that many also aren't aware of the qualities that contribute to credibility.

They need to demonstrate their *character*—the intention to do the right thing. This is of particular importance to subordinates, who tend to analyze every statement and nonverbal gesture for signs of the new boss's motives. Such scrutiny can be unnerving. "I knew I was a good guy, and I kind of expected people to accept me immediately for what I was," says one new manager. "But folks were wary, and you really had to earn it."

They need to demonstrate their *competence*—knowing how to do the right thing. This can be problematic, because new managers initially feel the need to prove their technical knowledge and prowess, the foundations of their success as individual performers. But while evidence of technical competence is important in gaining subordinates' respect, it isn't ultimately the primary area of competence that direct reports are looking for.

When Peter Isenberg took over the management of a trading desk in a global investment bank, he oversaw a group of seasoned, senior traders. To establish his credibility, he adopted a hands-on approach, advising traders to close down particular positions or try different trading strategies. The traders pushed back, demanding to know the rationale for each directive. Things got uncomfortable. The traders' responses to their new boss's comments became prickly and terse. One day, Isenberg, who recognized his lack of knowledge about foreign markets, asked one of the senior people a simple question about pricing. The trader stopped what he was doing for several minutes to explain the issue and offered to discuss the matter further at the end of the day. "Once I stopped talking all the time and began to listen, people on the desk started to educate me about the job and, significantly, seemed to question my calls far less," Isenberg says.

The new manager's eagerness to show off his technical competence had undermined his credibility as a manager and leader. His eagerness to jump in and try to solve problems raised implicit questions about his managerial competence. In the traders' eyes, he was becoming a micromanager and a "control freak" who didn't deserve their respect.

Finally, new managers need to demonstrate their *influence*—the ability to deliver and execute the right thing. There is "nothing worse than working for a powerless boss," says a direct report of one new manager I studied. Gaining and wielding influence within the organization is particularly difficult because, as I have noted, new managers are the "little bosses" of the organization. "I was on top of the world when I knew I was finally getting promoted," one new manager says. "I felt like I would be on the top of the ladder I had been climbing for years. But then I suddenly felt like I was at the bottom again—except this time it's not even clear what the rungs are and where I am climbing to."

Once again, we see a new manager fall into the trap of relying too heavily on his formal authority as his source of influence. Instead, he needs to build his influence by creating a web of strong, interdependent relationships, based on credibility and trust, throughout his team and the entire organization—one strand at a time.

Managers must control their direct reports

Most new managers, in part because of insecurity in an unfamiliar role, yearn for compliance from their subordinates. They fear that if they don't establish this early on, their direct reports will walk all over them. As a means of gaining this control, they often rely too much on their formal authority—a technique whose effectiveness is, as we have seen, questionable at best.

But even if they are able to achieve some measure of control, whether through formal authority or authority earned over time, they have achieved a false victory. Compliance does not equal commitment. If people aren't committed, they won't take the initiative. And if subordinates aren't taking the initiative, the manager can't delegate effectively. The direct reports won't take the calculated risks that lead to the continuous change and improvement required by today's turbulent business environment.

Winona Finch, who led the launch of the teen magazine in Latin America, knew she faced a business challenge that would require her team's total support. She had in fact been awarded the job in part because of her personal style, which her superiors hoped would compensate for her lack of experience in the Latin American market and in managing profit-and-loss responsibilities. In addition to being known as a clear thinker, she had a warm and personable way with people. During the project, she successfully leveraged these natural abilities in developing her leadership philosophy and style.

Instead of relying on formal authority to get what she wanted from her team, she exercised influence by creating a culture of inquiry. The result was an organization in which people felt empowered, committed, and accountable for fulfilling the company's vision. "Winona was easygoing and fun," a subordinate says. "But she would ask and ask and ask to get to the bottom of something. You would say something to her, she would say it back to you, and that way everyone was 100% clear on what we were talking about. Once she got the information and knew what you were doing, you had to be consistent. She would say, 'You told me X; why are you doing Y? I'm confused.'" Although she was demanding, she didn't demand that people do things her way. Her subordinates were committed to the team's goals because they were empowered, not ordered, to achieve them.

The more power managers are willing to share with subordinates in this way, the more influence they tend to command. When they lead in a manner that allows their people to take the initiative, they build their own credibility as managers.

Managers must focus on forging good individual relationships
Managing interdependencies and exercising informal authority derived from personal credibility require new managers to build trust, influence, and mutual expectations with a wide array of people. This is often achieved by establishing productive personal relationships. Ultimately, however, the new manager must figure out how to harness the power of a team. Simply focusing on one-on-one relationships with members of the team can undermine that process.

During their first year on the job, many new managers fail to recognize, much less address, their team-building responsibilities. Instead, they conceive of their people-management role as building the most effective relationships they can with each individual subordinate, erroneously equating the management of their team with managing the individuals on the team.

They attend primarily to individual performance and pay little or no attention to team culture and performance. They hardly ever rely on group forums for identifying and solving problems. Some spend too much time with a small number of trusted subordinates, often those who seem most supportive. New managers tend to handle issues, even those with teamwide implications, one-on-one. This leads them to make decisions based on unnecessarily limited information.

In his first week as a sales manager at a Texas software company, Roger Collins was asked by a subordinate for an assigned parking spot that had just become available. The salesman had been at the company for years, and Collins, wanting to get off to a good start with this veteran, said, "Sure, why not?" Within the hour, another salesman, a big moneymaker, stormed into Collins's office threatening to quit. It seems the shaded parking spot was coveted for pragmatic and symbolic reasons, and the beneficiary of Collins's casual gesture was widely viewed as incompetent. The manager's decision was unfathomable to the star.

Collins eventually solved what he regarded as a trivial management problem—"This is not the sort of thing I'm supposed to be worrying about," he said—but he began to recognize that every decision about individuals affected the team. He had been working on the assumption that if he could establish a good relationship with each person who reported to him, his whole team would function smoothly. What he learned was that supervising each individual was not the same as leading the team. In my research, I repeatedly hear new managers describe situations in which they made an exception for one subordinate—usually with the aim of creating a positive relationship with that person—but ended up regretting the action's unexpected negative consequences for the team. Grasping this notion can be especially difficult for up-and-comers who have been able to accomplish a great deal on their own.

When new managers focus solely on one-on-one relationships, they neglect a fundamental aspect of effective leadership: harnessing the collective power of the group to improve individual performance and commitment. By shaping team culture—the group's norms and values—a leader can unleash the problem-solving prowess of the diverse talents that make up the team.

Managers must ensure that things run smoothly

Like many managerial myths, this one is partly true but is misleading because it tells only some of the story. Making sure an operation is operating smoothly is an incredibly difficult task, requiring a manager to keep countless balls in the air at all times. Indeed, the complexity of maintaining the status quo can absorb all of a junior manager's time and energy.

But new managers also need to realize they are responsible for recommending and initiating changes that will enhance their groups' performance. Often—and it comes as a surprise to most—this means

Oh, One More Thing: Create the Conditions for Your Success

NEW MANAGERS OFTEN DISCOVER, BELATEDLY, that they are expected to do more than just make sure their groups function smoothly today. They must also recommend and initiate changes that will help their groups do even better in the future.

A new marketing manager at a telecommunications company whom I'll call John Delhorne discovered that his predecessor had failed to make critical investments, so he tried on numerous occasions to convince his immediate superior to increase the marketing budget. He also presented a proposal to acquire a new information system that could allow his team to optimize its marketing initiatives. When he could not persuade his boss to release more money, he hunkered down and focused on changes within his team that would make it as productive as possible under the circumstances. This course seemed prudent, especially because his relationship with his boss, who was taking longer and longer to answer Delhorne's e-mails, was becoming strained.

When the service failed to meet certain targets, the CEO unceremoniously fired Delhorne because, Delhorne was told, he hadn't been proactive. The CEO chastised Delhorne for "sitting back and not asking for his help" in securing the funds needed to succeed in a critical new market. Delhorne, shocked and hurt, thought the CEO was being grossly unfair. Delhorne contended it wasn't his fault that the company's strategic-planning and budgeting procedures were flawed. The CEO's response: It was Delhorne's responsibility to create the conditions for his success.

---

challenging organizational processes or structures that exist above and beyond their area of formal authority. Only when they understand this part of the job will they begin to address seriously their leadership responsibilities. (See the sidebar "Oh, One More Thing: Create the Conditions for Your Success.")

In fact, most new managers see themselves as targets of organizational change initiatives, implementing with their groups the changes ordered from above. They don't see themselves as change agents. Hierarchical thinking and their fixation on the authority that comes with being the boss lead them to define their responsibilities too narrowly. Consequently, they tend to blame flawed systems, and the superiors directly responsible for those systems, for their teams' setbacks—and they tend to wait for other people to fix the problems.

But this represents a fundamental misunderstanding of their role within the organization. New managers need to generate changes, both within *and outside* their areas of responsibility, to ensure that their teams can succeed. They need to work to change the context in which their teams operate, ignoring their lack of formal authority.

This broader view benefits the organization as well as the new manager. Organizations must continually revitalize and transform themselves. They can meet these challenges only if they have cadres of effective leaders capable of both managing the complexity of the status quo and initiating change.

New Managers Aren't Alone

As they go through the daunting process of becoming a boss, new managers can gain a tremendous advantage by learning to recognize the misconceptions I've just outlined. But given the multilayered nature of their new responsibilities, they are still going to make mistakes as they try to put together the managerial puzzle—and making mistakes, no matter how important to the learning process, is no fun. They are going to feel pain as their professional identities are stretched and reshaped. As they struggle to learn a new role, they will often feel isolated.

Unfortunately, my research has shown that few new managers ask for help. This is in part the outcome of yet another misconception: The boss is supposed to have all the answers, so seeking help is a sure sign that a new manager is a "promotion mistake." Of course, seasoned managers know that no one has all the answers. The insights a manager does possess come over time, through experience. And, as countless studies show, it is easier to learn on the job if you can draw on the support and assistance of peers and superiors.

Another reason new managers don't seek help is that they perceive the dangers (sometimes more imagined than real) of forging developmental relationships. When you share your anxieties, mistakes, and shortcomings with peers in your part of the organization, there's a risk that the individuals will use that information against you. The same goes for sharing your problems with your superior. The inherent conflict between the roles of evaluator and developer is an age-old dilemma. So new managers need to be creative in finding support. For instance, they might seek out peers who are outside their region or function or in another organization altogether. The problem with bosses, while difficult to solve neatly, can be alleviated. And herein lies a lesson not only for new managers but for experienced bosses, as well.

The new manager avoids turning to her immediate superior for advice because she sees that person as a threat to, rather than an ally in, her development. Because she fears punishment for missteps and failures, she resists seeking the help that might prevent such mistakes, even when she's desperate for it. As one new manager reports:

"I know on one level that I should deal more with my manager because that is what he is there for. He's got the experience, and I probably owe it to him to go to him and tell him what's up. He would probably have some good advice. But it's not safe to share with him. He's an unknown quantity. If you ask too many questions, he may lose confidence in you and think things aren't going very well. He may see that you are a little bit out of control, and then you really have a tough job. Because he'll be down there lickety-split, asking lots of questions about what you are doing, and before you know it, he'll be involved right in the middle of it. That's a really uncomfortable situation. He's the last place I'd go for help."

Such fears are often justified. Many a new manager has regretted trying to establish a mentoring relationship with his boss. "I don't dare even ask a question that could be perceived as naive or stupid," says one. "Once I asked him a question and he made me feel like I was a kindergartner in the business. It was as if he had said, 'That was the dumbest thing I've ever seen. What on earth did you have in mind?'"

This is a tragically lost opportunity for the new manager, the boss, and the organization as a whole. It means that the new manager's boss loses a chance to influence the manager's initial conceptions and misconceptions of her new position and how she should approach it. The new manager loses the chance to draw on organizational assets—from financial resources to information about senior management's priorities—that the superior could best provide.

When a new manager can develop a good relationship with his boss, it can make all the difference in the world—though not necessarily in ways the new manager expects. My research suggests that eventually about half of new managers turn to their bosses for assistance, often because of a looming crisis. Many are relieved to find their superiors more tolerant of their questions and mistakes than they had expected. "He recognized that I was still in the learning mode and was more than willing to help in any way he could," recalls one new manager.

Sometimes, the most expert mentors can seem deceptively hands-off. One manager reports how she learned from an immediate superior: "She is demanding, but she enjoys a reputation for growing people and helping them, not throwing them to the wolves. I wasn't sure after the first 60 days, though. Everything was so hard and I was so frustrated, but she didn't offer to help. It was driving me nuts. When I asked her a question, she asked me a question. I got no answers. Then I saw what she wanted. I had to come in with some ideas about how I would handle the situation, and then she would talk about them with me. She would spend all the time in the world with me."

His experience vividly highlights why it's important for the bosses of new managers to understand—or simply recall—how difficult it is to step into a management role for the first time. Helping a new manager succeed doesn't benefit only that individual. Ensuring the new manager's success is also crucially important to the success of the entire organization.

Originally published in January 2007. Reprint 7251

Leading the Team You Inherit

by Michael D. Watkins

DAVID BENET HAD PROBLEMS TO SOLVE when he came in to lead the highest-growth unit at a large medical devices company. Although sales had increased when two new products launched the previous year, the numbers still fell short of expectations, given all the evidence of unmet customer needs. The company's future hinged on the success of both products—an instrument for inserting stents into blocked arteries and an electronic implant for stabilizing cardiac rhythm.

So the long-term stakes were high, and the team wasn't exactly humming. Stories about missed opportunities and hints of a toxic culture had drifted upward to senior management.

All those factors had prompted the decision to replace the unit's executive vice president with someone from the outside, and David fit the bill. He had a record of stellar accomplishments at a rival company, where he had turned around one business unit and accelerated the growth of another. But in taking on this new role, he faced a common challenge: He didn't get to handpick the people who would be working with him. Rather, he inherited his predecessor's team— the team that had created the situation David was hired to fix.

Indeed, most newly appointed leaders have limited familiarity with their teams at the outset and can't immediately swap in new people to help grow or transform the business. Sometimes they lack the necessary political power or resources to rapidly replace personnel, or the culture does not allow it. Often, existing team members are essential for running the business in the short term but not the right people to lead it into the future.

All this highlights the importance of figuring out how to work effectively with a team you have inherited. Fraught with trade-offs, the process is like repairing an airplane in midflight. You can't just shut down the plane's engines while you rebuild them—at least not without causing a crash. You need to maintain stability while moving ahead.

There are many frameworks to help leaders build new teams. One of the best known is "forming, storming, norming, and performing," created by Bruce Tuckman in 1965. According to Tuckman's model and more recent ones like it, teams go through predictable phases of development that, with the right interventions, can be accelerated. The problem is that these models assume leaders build their teams from scratch, carefully choosing members and setting direction from the very beginning.

In my work helping leaders navigate major transitions, I have found that most people, like David, instead need a framework for taking over and transforming a team. That's what this article provides. First, leaders must assess the human capital and group dynamics they have inherited, to get a clear picture of the current state. Next, they must reshape the team according to what's needed—looking with fresh eyes at its membership, sense of purpose and direction, operating model, and behavioral patterns. Finally, they can accelerate team development and improve performance by identifying opportunities for early wins and making plans to secure them.

Assessing the Team

When you are leading a new team, you must quickly determine whether you have the right people doing the right things in the right ways to propel the organization forward. From day one you will

Idea in Brief

What's Wrong

Most team-building frameworks assume that you get to cherry-pick members and set the direction and tone from day one. But leaders usually don't have that luxury; they must work with the people they inherit.

What's Needed

Leaders who are taking over and transforming a team need guidance on how to navigate the transition and improve performance.

What's Effective

Here's a three-step model that works: First, assess the people you've got and the dynamics at play. Second, reshape the team's membership, sense of purpose and direction, operating model, and behaviors according to the business challenges you face. Third, accelerate the team's development by scoring some early wins.

have a lot of demands on your time and attention, and those will only grow, so efficient team assessment is key.

It's important to be systematic, as well. Although most leaders inherit and size up many teams over their careers, few are deliberate about what they look for in people. Through experience they arrive at intuitive assessment criteria and methods—which are fine for familiar situations but otherwise problematic. Why? Because the characteristics of effective team members vary dramatically depending on the circumstances.

Your assessments will be faster and more accurate if you explicitly state your criteria. What qualities should people have in order to tackle the particular challenges your team faces? How important are diverse or complementary skills in the group? Which attributes do you think you can shape through your leadership? You may be able to improve people's engagement and focus, for example, but not their inherent trustworthiness. (See the sidebar "What Qualities Are You Looking For?")

Your requirements will depend partly on the state of the business. In a turnaround, you will seek people who are already up to speed—you won't have time to focus on skill building until things are more stable. If you are trying to sustain a team's success, however, it

What Qualities Are You Looking For?

LIKE MOST LEADERS, YOU MAY have a "gut" sense of what you typically look for in people. But different situations and challenges call for different strengths. This exercise will help you better understand and articulate your priorities each time you inherit a team.

Assign percentages to the qualities below, according to how much emphasis you think each should receive, given your current circumstances and goals. Make sure the numbers in the right column add up to 100.

Those numbers will be rough, of course. For some team members (say, your head of finance), competence may be the top priority; for others (say, your head of marketing), energy or people skills may be equally or more critical. The importance of the role and the state of the business may also affect your estimates.

When executives complete this exercise, they almost always give trustworthiness the most weight. That's because they view it as a sign of inherent character—not something that can be strengthened with good management. However, leaders do think they can help team members improve their focus and energy. So it's not surprising that they give those qualities less emphasis than trustworthiness early on.

What do your rankings say about what you value most right now and what you believe you can influence through leadership? Are any of the criteria go/no-go issues for you?

---

probably makes sense to develop high potentials, and you will have more time to do so.

Your expectations for team members will also be shaped by how essential their roles are to meeting your goals. People in critical positions will be assessed with greater urgency and higher standards. David Benet (names are disguised throughout) had two sales leaders, both deemed critical because their groups had to drive cardiologists' awareness of the new products. They both needed to be immediately effective at communicating the products' benefits to opinion leaders. The head of HR was a vital role, too—serious midlevel talent weaknesses in sales and marketing had to be addressed soon. The head of communications, however, wasn't as big a priority; reviews

Quality	Description	Importance
Competence	Has the technical expertise and experience to do the job effectively	
Trustworthiness	Can be relied upon to be straight with you and to follow through on commitments	
Energy	Brings the right attitude to the job (isn't burned-out or disengaged)	
People skills	Gets along well with others on the team and supports collaboration	
Focus	Sets priorities and sticks to them, instead of veering off in all directions	
Judgment	Exercises good sense, especially under pressure or when faced with making sacrifices for the greater good	
TOTAL		100 percent

of his work and conversations with colleagues revealed that he could be more innovative, but David decided to leave him in place for the time being.

Another factor to consider is to what degree your reports need to work as a team, and on what tasks. Ask yourself, "Will the people I supervise have to collaborate a lot, or is it OK if they operate mostly independently?" The answer will help determine how important it is for you to cultivate teamwork. Think of the people who typically report to a corporate treasurer, such as the heads of tax, cash management, and M&A analysis. These individuals should strive to operate as a high-performing group of managers who run their departments independently and effectively. Trying to turn that

Sizing Up People One-on-One

EARLY ONE-ON-ONE MEETINGS are a valuable tool for assessing the members of your new team. Depending on your style, these meetings might be informal discussions, formal reviews, or a combination, but you should approach them in a standard way.

Prepare

Review available personnel history, performance data, and appraisals. Familiarize yourself with each person's skills so that you can assess how he functions on the team and with his own unit or group. Observe how team members interact. Do relations appear cordial and productive? Tense and competitive? Explain to everyone that you will be using the meetings to assess the whole team and individual members.

Create an Interview Template

Ask people the same questions, and see how their insights vary. For example, What are the strengths and weaknesses of our existing strategy? What are our biggest challenges and opportunities in the short term? In the medium term? What resources could we leverage more effectively? How could we improve the way the team works together? If you were in my position, what would your priorities be?

---

group into a team through classic activities like creating a shared vision and establishing common performance goals and metrics would just frustrate everyone, because little or no collaborative work needs to be done. In such situations, assessment and management would focus more on individual performance and less on ability to work together. David, however, had a team of functional leaders who were quite interdependent. For example, he needed his VPs of sales, marketing, and communications to work closely together on refining and executing go-to-market strategies for the two products. So he had to gauge their relationships and collaborative capabilities.

To conduct an effective assessment, you'll hold a mix of one-on-one and team meetings, supplementing with input from key stakeholders such as customers, suppliers, and colleagues outside the team. (See the sidebar "Sizing Up People One-on-One.") You'll

Look for Verbal and Nonverbal Clues

Notice what people say and don't say. Do they volunteer information, or do you have to extract it? Do they take responsibility for problems, make excuses, or point fingers at others? You should also look for inconsistencies between people's words and their body language. That sort of mismatch can signal dishonesty or distrust of management—and either way, it needs to be addressed. Pay attention as well to topics that elicit strong emotions. Those hot buttons provide clues about what motivates people and what kinds of changes would energize them.

Summarize and Share What You Learn

After you've interviewed everyone, discuss your findings with the team. This will demonstrate that you are coming up to speed quickly. If your feedback highlights differences of opinion or raises uncomfortable issues, you'll also have a chance to observe the team under a modest amount of stress. Watching how people respond may lead to valuable insight into team culture and power dynamics.

also look at team members' individual track records and performance evaluations. Those didn't turn up any immediate red flags for David—but he knew the team had underperformed. His meetings helped him determine why and what to do about it.

It soon became clear that he had two significant personnel issues. The first was Carlos, the VP of surgical sales. Carlos had the longest tenure with the company and a seemingly tight connection with the CEO. However, his performance on the new surgical product had been lackluster. More important, comments from his peers and direct reports pointed to a micromanaging leadership style that undermined morale in his group and revealed a lack of collaboration with the rest of the team. For instance, he was hoarding information that could have been valuable to the interventional sales group and to the marketing people, and this was poisoning team dynamics.

Henry, the VP of human resources, presented a different challenge. He would have been a solid HR leader in normal circumstances, because he was skilled at handling typical challenges associated with hiring, performance management, and compensation and benefits. But he was not well suited to the demands of a high-growth environment. David reviewed the work Henry had done on talent appraisal and succession planning and rated it a B at best.

After completing his assessment, David decided that he would retain most of his team members, whose tenure with the company varied from five years to more than 25. But he knew he had to work on people's attitudes—especially the lack of trust between functions.

Reshaping the Team

Post-assessment, the next task is to reshape the team within the constraints of the organization's culture, the leader's mandate, and the available talent. Ultimately new leaders want their people to exhibit high-performance behaviors such as sharing information freely, identifying and dealing with conflict swiftly, solving problems creatively, supporting one another, and presenting a unified face to the outside world once decisions have been made. Leaders can promote these behaviors by focusing on four factors: the team's composition, its alignment with a shared vision, its operating model, and its integration of new rules and expectations.

Composition

The most obvious way to reshape a team is to replace underperformers and anyone whose capabilities are not a good match for the situation. But this can be difficult culturally and politically, and in many cases, it's simply not possible—leaders must work with the people they inherit. Even when employees can be let go and newcomers brought in, the process takes time and consumes energy. So doing this in the first few months should be reserved for dire business situations, for employees in critical roles who clearly cannot do the work, or for truly toxic personalities that are undermining the enterprise.

Fortunately, you can reshape team composition in other ways. For instance, you might wait for normal turnover to create space for the types of people you want. This usually takes time, but you may be able to speed up the process by signaling your expectations of higher performance—thus encouraging marginal performers to seek other roles. You can also watch for positions in other areas of the organization that might suit people who are valuable but not a good match for your team.

Another option is to groom high potentials to take on new responsibilities, provided you have enough time and other resources. If not, you may instead choose to alter individuals' roles to better match their capabilities. This powerful, often underappreciated way of reshaping teams may involve adjusting the scope of existing roles, having people swap jobs, or creating new positions by carving up the work differently. Any of these tactics can revitalize people who have become stale in their jobs, but few leaders think of trying alternative ways of allocating work.

David used a mix of these approaches to change the composition of his team. He concluded that Carlos, the VP of surgical sales, was undermining effectiveness and needed to leave. After consulting with senior management and corporate HR, David offered him a generous early retirement package, eliminated his role, and restructured the sales groups under a single VP. He appointed Carlos's counterpart in interventional sales, Lois, to lead the unified sales organization. To help Lois succeed in the bigger role, David asked HR to enroll her in an intensive leadership development program that included coaching.

David's other major move on personnel was to find a new position in the company for Henry, his VP of human resources. Fortunately, the corporate compensation and benefits group had an opening that was a great fit, and Henry gladly took it, feeling somewhat burned out from the stresses David's unit had experienced. That allowed David to search for a new VP with the talent planning, acquisition, and development capabilities needed to strengthen the lower levels of the sales and marketing organizations.

Alignment

You will also need to ensure that everyone has a clear sense of purpose and direction. Sometimes a team's stated direction needs to be changed. In other cases, it's more or less right, but people are just not pulling together.

To get everyone aligned, the team must agree on answers to four basic questions:

What will we accomplish? You spell this out in your mission, goals, and key metrics.

Why should we do it? Here is where your vision statement and incentives come into play.

How will we do it? This includes defining the team's strategy in relation to the organization's, as well as sorting out the plans and activities needed for execution.

Who will do what? People's roles and responsibilities must support all of the above.

Generally leaders are more comfortable with alignment than with other aspects of reshaping, because they have well-established tools and processes for tackling it. But one element in particular tends to trip them up: the "why." If the team lacks a clear and compelling vision that inspires them, and if members lack the proper incentives, they probably won't move energetically in the right direction. Compensation and benefits aren't sufficient motivators on their own. You need to offer a full set of rewards, including interesting work, status, and potential for advancement.

This can be challenging, for a couple of reasons: It's often hard to discern when *hidden* incentives (like competing commitments to other teams) are getting in the way. And you may have limited influence on certain rewards, as is often the case with compensation.

During individual assessment interviews and in group discussions, David had discovered that people weren't as aligned on goals, metrics, and incentives as they needed to be. Specifically, the two sales forces had no incentives to help each other. In addition, the marketing teams for the two products were underresourced and competing for available funding in dysfunctional ways.

To get his team members striving for the same things, David worked with them to develop a comprehensive dashboard of metrics that could be reviewed on a regular basis. He also realigned the team with the rest of the company by raising the performance bar to match the executive committee's expectations. In the business planning process, he committed the team to achieving a higher level of growth. Perhaps most important, he addressed the issue of misaligned incentives that had created conflict between the two sales groups. With that function now unified, he and Lois restructured the sales force on a geographic basis so that individual salespeople represented both of the new products and were rewarded accordingly.

Operating model

Reshaping a team also involves rethinking how and when people come together to do the work. This may include increasing or decreasing the number of "core" members, creating subteams, adjusting the types and frequency of meetings, running meetings differently, and designing new protocols for follow-up.

Such changes can be powerful levers for improving team performance. Unfortunately, many new leaders either continue to operate the way their predecessors did or make only small adjustments. To think more creatively about your team's operating model, identify your real constraints on how the work gets done—such as established business planning and budgeting processes for the entire enterprise—and then ask yourself how the team could operate within them more efficiently and productively. In addition, consider whether it makes sense to create subteams (formal or informal) to improve collaboration among interdependent members. Also think about whether certain activities require more-frequent attention than others. This will help you establish a meeting cadence that works, both for the team as a whole and for any subteams.

David recognized key interdependencies among sales, marketing, and communications, so he set up a subteam of leaders from those functions. To get more-focused attention and faster feedback from them, he decided to meet with them weekly, while holding full-team meetings only every other month and reserving those for information sharing and discussion of strategic issues. The subteam oversaw efforts to refine and execute go-to-market strategies for the two products—David's immediate priority. The work was done by cross-functional teams consisting of the sales, marketing, and communications leaders' direct reports. Streamlining processes, increasing collaboration, and speeding up reaction times—combined with the restructuring of the sales force and additional funding for the marketing teams—rapidly increased sales growth.

When rethinking meeting frequency and agendas, it helps to understand the three types of meetings that leadership teams typically have—strategic, operational, and learning—so that you can allocate an appropriate amount of time to each. *Strategic* meetings concern the biggest decisions that need to be made—about business models, vision, strategy, organizational configurations, and so on. Though they tend to be relatively infrequent, they require time for in-depth discussion. *Operational* meetings involve reviewing forecasts and measures of short-term performance, and adjusting activities and plans in light of those results. These are usually shorter and more frequent than strategic meetings. *Learning* meetings are scheduled on an as-needed basis, often after crises or in response to emerging issues. They can also focus on team building.

When teams try to jam all these activities into a single recurring meeting, operational urgencies tend to crowd out strategic and learning discussions. By thinking through the right mix of meeting types and scheduling each kind on its own regular cycle, you can prevent that problem. It's typically best to work out a rhythm for your operational meetings first, deciding how frequent they should be and who should participate. Then you can overlay the less-frequent strategic meetings, allowing plenty of time for discussion. Finally, you should establish what kinds of events will trigger the ad hoc learning meetings. You might, for example, decide to hold them after any major market event, such as the introduction of a competing product, or in the wake of a significant internal failure, such as a product recall.

Integration

The final element of reshaping is integration. This involves establishing ground rules and processes to feed and sustain desired behaviors and serving as a role model for your team members. Of course, the team's composition, alignment, and operating model also influence members' behavior. But focusing on those elements isn't sufficient, especially when leaders inherit teams with negative group dynamics. Those situations require remedial work: changing the destructive patterns of behavior and fostering a sense of shared purpose.

That was the case with David's team. The infighting between the marketing and sales VPs, combined with the previous leader's inability to curb Carlos's bad behavior or secure resources, had eroded members' trust. Once David restructured sales, the team realized that he was a decisive straight shooter (unlike his predecessor). He also earned respect with the changes he made in team membership and the funding he obtained for marketing. So he was in a good position to rebuild trust. He began by commissioning a more focused assessment of team dynamics; the time was right for a deeper dive on this, now that he had been in his role a bit longer and had established credibility with the group. This independent, expert evaluation included an anonymous survey of team members and follow-up interviews that zeroed in on the key elements of trust within leadership teams:

- confidence that all team members have the capabilities to do their jobs

- transparency in sharing information

- belief that commitments will be honored

- psychological safety to express divergent opinions without fear of belittlement, criticism, or retribution

- security that confidences will be maintained

- unity around decisions once people agree to them

The evaluation revealed that transparency, psychological safety, and unity were the primary trust issues for the team. To communicate those results, David brought everyone together for an offsite. He pointed out that they would never be a winning team if the trust problems persisted. He also shared what he had found to be the structural causes (misaligned incentives, underfunding, Carlos's impact) and what had already been done to address them. Crucially, he expressed confidence that the unit could become a high-performing team—and he voiced his commitment to making that happen.

David then laid out a process for reshaping group dynamics. First, everybody would agree on certain behavioral principles: They would share information, treat one another with respect, and act as "one team" after decisions were made. Then they would approach decision making with greater transparency. For each decision, he would communicate up front whether he would make the call, open it up to a small group, or seek full-team consensus.

After the offsite, David focused on "living" these new principles and processes himself. He also reinforced desired behaviors. And when he saw any unproductive behaviors emerge, he intervened immediately—either in team meetings or privately with individuals. Although it took time, because old habits die hard, the group dynamics improved.

David was careful to revisit these principles and processes when his new VP of HR joined the team. Revisiting and reinforcing behavioral expectations should be standard practice any time there is a change in team membership or mission. It's also valuable to schedule a regular (quarterly or semiannual) review of how the team is functioning and whether the principles are being upheld.

Accelerating the Team's Development

Building on their assessment and reshaping work, leaders need to energize team members with some early wins. As David knew from experience, this increases people's confidence in their capabilities and reinforces the value of their new rules and processes. He and his team started by setting challenging goals for the next three months' sales; then they set about delivering. They specified the work involved and who was accountable for it, determined which external stakeholders' support was essential, allocated responsibility for building relationships, and developed messages and methods for sharing results with the rest of the organization. They exceeded their goals by a substantial margin.

Once the team had those successes in place, it kept building on them. The result was a virtuous cycle of achievement and confidence. By the end of David's first year, sales growth had far outstripped targets. In fact, already-ambitious forecasts had to be revised upward three times. The executive committee was understandably delighted by the progress, which created an opening for David to secure additional resources, expand the sales force, and exceed the usual salary limits to hire outstanding talent. The growth trajectory continued for the next two years, until competitors' introductions of new products began to make things more challenging. By that time, however, David's team had achieved a dominant position in the market, and it was ready to launch new products of its own.

Originally published in June 2016. Reprint R1606D

Saving Your Rookie Managers from Themselves

by Carol A. Walker

TOM EDELMAN, LIKE A MILLION freshly minted managers before him, had done a marvelous job as an individual contributor. He was smart, confident, forward thinking, and resourceful. His clients liked him, as did his boss and coworkers. Consequently, no one in the department was surprised when his boss offered him a managerial position. Tom accepted with some ambivalence—he loved working directly with clients and was loath to give that up—but on balance, he was thrilled.

Six months later, when I was called in to coach Tom (I've disguised his name), I had trouble even picturing the confident insider he once had been. He looked like a deer caught in the headlights. Tom seemed overwhelmed and indeed even used that word several times to describe how he felt. He had started to doubt his abilities. His direct reports, once close colleagues, no longer seemed to respect or even like him. What's more, his department had been beset by a series of small crises, and Tom spent most of his time putting out these fires. He knew this wasn't the most effective use of his time, but he didn't know how to stop. These problems hadn't yet translated into poor business results, but he was in trouble nonetheless.

His boss realized that he was in danger of failing and brought me in to assist. With support and coaching, Tom got the help he needed and eventually became an effective manager. Indeed, he has been promoted twice since I worked with him, and he now runs a small division within the same company. But his near failure—and the path that brought him to that point—is surprisingly typical. Most organizations promote employees into managerial positions based on their technical competence. Very often, however, those people fail to grasp how their roles have changed—that their jobs are no longer about personal achievement but instead about enabling others to achieve, that sometimes driving the bus means taking a backseat, and that building a team is often more important than cutting a deal. Even the best employees can have trouble adjusting to these new realities. That trouble may be exacerbated by normal insecurities that make rookie managers hesitant to ask for help, even when they find themselves in thoroughly unfamiliar territory. As these new managers internalize their stress, their focus becomes internal as well. They become insecure and self-focused and cannot properly support their teams. Inevitably, trust breaks down, staff members are alienated, and productivity suffers.

Many companies unwittingly support this downward spiral by assuming that their rookie managers will somehow learn critical management skills by osmosis. Some rookies do, to be sure, but in my experience they're the exceptions. Most need more help. In the absence of comprehensive training and intensive coaching—which most companies don't offer—the rookie manager's boss plays a key role. Of course, it's not possible for most senior managers to spend hours and hours every week overseeing a new manager's work, but if you know what typical challenges a rookie manager faces, you'll be able to anticipate some problems before they arise and nip others in the bud.

Delegating

Effective delegation may be one of the most difficult tasks for rookie managers. Senior managers bestow on them big responsibilities and tight deadlines, and they put a lot of pressure on them to produce

Idea in Brief

You've wisely promoted a top performer into management. Six months later, this rising star has fallen hard: He's overwhelmed, fearful, not respected by his staff. Why?

You probably promoted him based on his technical competence—then expected him to learn management skills by osmosis.

But he didn't grasp the real challenges of management—for example, empowering others versus striving for personal achievement. Insecure about asking for help, he turned inward. His team's morale plummeted; productivity faltered.

How to save your erstwhile star? Help him master delegating, thinking strategically, and communicating—basic skills that trip up *most* new managers.

results. The natural response of rookies when faced with such challenges is to "just do it," thinking that's what got them promoted in the first place. But their reluctance to delegate assignments also has its roots in some very real fears. First is the fear of losing stature: If I assign high-profile projects to my staff members, they'll get the credit. What kind of visibility will I be left with? Will it be clear to my boss and my staff what value I'm adding? Second is the fear of abdicating control: If I allow Frank to do this, how can I be sure that he will do it correctly? In the face of this fear, the rookie manager may delegate tasks but supervise Frank so closely that he will never feel accountable. Finally, the rookie may be hesitant to delegate work because he's afraid of overburdening his staff. He may be uncomfortable assigning work to former peers for fear that they'll resent him. But the real resentment usually comes when staff members feel that lack of opportunity is blocking their advancement.

Signs that these fears may be playing out include new managers who work excessively long hours, are hesitant to take on new responsibilities, have staff members who seem unengaged, or have a tendency to answer on behalf of employees instead of encouraging them to communicate with you directly.

The first step toward helping young managers delegate effectively is to get them to understand their new role. Acknowledge that

Idea in Practice

Essential management skills for rookie managers:

Delegating. Under pressure to produce, rookies often "just do it" themselves because they fear losing control or overburdening others. But failure to delegate blocks their staffs' advancement, making them resentful, and then disengaged.

How to help:

- Explain that developing staff is *as* essential as financial achievements.

- Lead by example. Trust and empower your rookie; he'll engage his *own* team.

- Encourage him to take small risks in playing to his staff's strengths. Early successes will build his confidence.

- Help him break complex projects into manageable chunks with clear milestones.

Getting support from above. Many rookie managers believe they're in servitude to bosses, not in partnership. To avoid seeming vulnerable, they don't ask for help. But if they don't see you as a critical support source, they won't see *themselves* as one for their team.

How to help:

- Emphasize that open communication is essential to your rookie's success. Discourage covering up problems.

- Introduce him to other managers as resources.

- Have *him* prepare agendas for your regular meetings. The process will help him organize his thoughts.

Projecting confidence. Rookies who don't project confidence won't energize their teams. Frantic, arrogant, or insecure demeanors may repel others in the company.

How to help:

- Encourage "conscious comportment": constant awareness

their job fundamentally differs from an individual contributor's. Clarify what you and the organization value in leaders. Developing talented, promotable staff is critical in any company. Let new managers know that they will be rewarded for these less tangible efforts in addition to hitting numerical goals. Understanding this new role is half the battle for rookie managers, and one that many companies mistakenly assume is evident from the start.

of the image your rookie is projecting.

- Let him express his feelings— but in your office, behind closed doors.

- Keep him from undermining his own authority; e.g., by pushing an initiative only because top management requested it. Walk through the process of presenting an initiative persuasively, ensuring he can *own* the message—not just deliver it.

Focusing on the big picture. Many rookie managers let fire fighting eclipse strategic initiatives. Fire fighting *feels* productive—but it doesn't teach teams to handle challenges themselves or think strategically.

How to help:

- Explain that strategic thinking will constitute more of your rookie's work as his career advances.

- Help him focus on the long-term, big picture. Ask strategic questions; e.g., "What marketplace trends are you seeing that could affect you in six months?"

- Request written plans documenting strategic goals as well as concrete, supporting actions.

Giving constructive feedback. Most rookies dread correcting staffers' inadequate performance. But avoidance costs managers their credibility.

How to help:

- Explain that constructive feedback strengthens staffers' skills.

- Role-play giving feedback about behaviors, not personalities.

After clarifying how your rookie manager's role has changed, you can move on to tactics. Perhaps it goes without saying, but you should lead by example. You have the responsibility to empower the rookie who works for you and do what you can to help him overcome his insecurities about his value to the organization. You can then assist him in looking for opportunities to empower and engage his team.

One young manager I worked with desperately needed to find time to train and supervise new employees. His firm had been recently acquired, and he had to deal with high staff turnover and new industrywide rules and regulations. The most senior person on his staff—a woman who had worked for the acquiring company—was about to return from an extended family leave, and he was convinced that he couldn't ask her for help. After all, she had a part-time schedule, and she'd asked to be assigned to the company's largest client. To complicate matters, he suspected that she resented his promotion. As we evaluated the situation, the manager was able to see that the senior staffer's number one priority was reestablishing herself as an important part of the team. Once he realized this, he asked her to take on critical supervisory responsibilities, balanced with a smaller client load, and she eagerly agreed. Indeed, she returned from leave excited about partnering with her manager to develop the team.

When a new manager grumbles about mounting workloads, seize the opportunity to discuss delegation. Encourage him to take small risks initially, playing to the obvious strengths of his staff members. Asking his super-organized, reliable assistant to take the lead in handling the logistics of a new product launch, for example, is much less risky than asking a star salesperson, unaccustomed to this sort of detailed work, to do it. Early successes will build the manager's confidence and willingness to take progressively larger risks in stretching each team member's capabilities. Reinforce to him that delegation does not mean abdication. Breaking a complex project into manageable chunks, each with clearly defined milestones, makes effective follow-up easier. It's also important to schedule regular meetings before the project even begins in order to ensure that the manager stays abreast of progress and that staff members feel accountable.

Getting Support from Above

Most first-time managers see their relationship with their boss more as one of servitude than of partnership. They will wait for you to initiate meetings, ask for reports, and question results. You may welcome this restraint, but generally it's a bad sign. For one thing, it puts undue pressure on you to keep the flow of communication going. Even more important, it prevents new managers from looking to you as a critical source of support. If they don't see you that way, it's unlikely that they will see themselves that way for their own people. The problem isn't only that your position intimidates them; it's also that they fear being vulnerable. A newly promoted manager doesn't want you to see weaknesses, lest you think you made a mistake in promoting her. When I ask rookie managers about their relationships with their bosses, they often admit that they are trying to "stay under the boss's radar" and are "careful about what [they] say to the boss."

Some inexperienced managers will not seek your help even when they start to founder. Seemingly capable rookie managers often try to cover up a failing project or relationship—just until they can get it back under control. For example, one manager I worked with at a technology company hired a professional 20 years her senior. The transition was rocky, and, despite her best efforts, the individual wasn't acclimating to the organization. (The company, like many in the technology sector, was very youth oriented.) Rather than reaching out to her boss for help, the manager continued to grapple with the situation alone. The staff member ultimately resigned at the busiest time of the year, and the young manager suffered the dual punishment of being understaffed at the worst possible moment and having it known that she had lost a potentially important contributor.

What's the boss of a rookie manager to do? You can begin by clarifying expectations. Explain the connection between the rookie's success and your success, so that she understands that open communication is necessary for you to achieve your goals. Explain that you don't expect her to have all the answers. Introduce her to other managers within the company who may be helpful, and encourage her to contact them as needed. Let her know that mistakes happen but that the cover-up is always worse than the crime. Let her know that you like to receive occasional lunch invitations as much as you like to extend them.

Lunch and drop-by meetings are important, but they usually aren't enough. Consider meeting regularly with a new manager—perhaps weekly in the early stages of a new assignment, moving to biweekly or monthly as her confidence builds. These meetings will develop rapport, provide you with insight into how the person is approaching the job, and make the new manager organize her thoughts on a regular basis. Be clear that the meetings are her time and that it's up to her to plan the agenda. You're there to ask and answer questions and to offer advice. The message you send is that the individual's work is important to you and that you're a committed business partner. More subtly, you're modeling how to simultaneously empower and guide direct reports.

Projecting Confidence

Looking confident when you don't feel confident—it's a challenge we all face, and as senior managers we're usually conscious of the need when it arises. Rookie managers are often so internally focused that they are unaware of this need or the image they project. They are so focused on substance that they forget that form counts, too. The first weeks and months on the job are a critical time for new leaders to reach out to staff. If they don't project confidence, they are unlikely to inspire and energize their teams.

I routinely work with new managers who are unaware that their everyday demeanor is hurting their organizations. In one rapidly growing technology company, the service manager, Linda, faced high levels of stress. Service outages were all too common, and they were beyond her control. Customers were exacting, and they too were under great pressure. Her rapidly growing staff was generally inexperienced. Distraught customers and employees had her tied up in knots almost daily. She consistently appeared breathless, rushed, and fearful that the other shoe was about to drop. The challenge was perhaps too big for a first-time manager, but that's what happens in rapidly growing companies. On one level, Linda was doing an excellent job keeping the operation going. The client base was growing and retention was certainly high—largely as a result of her energy and resourcefulness. But on another level, she was doing a lot of damage.

Linda's frantic demeanor had two critical repercussions. First, she had unwittingly defined the standard for acceptable conduct in her department, and her inexperienced staff began to display the same behaviors. Before long, other departments were reluctant to communicate with Linda or her team, for fear of bothering them or eliciting an emotional reaction. But for the company to arrive at real solutions to the service problems, departments needed to openly exchange information, and that wasn't happening. Second, Linda was not portraying herself to senior managers as promotion material. They were pleased with her troubleshooting abilities, but they did not see a confident, thoughtful senior manager in the making. The image Linda was projecting would ultimately hold back both her career and her department.

Not all rookie managers display the problems that Linda did. Some appear excessively arrogant. Others wear their self-doubt on their sleeves. Whether your managers appear overwhelmed, arrogant, or insecure, honest feedback is your best tool. You can help rookie managers by telling them that it's always safe to let out their feelings—in your office, behind closed doors. Reinforce just how long a shadow they cast once they assume leadership positions. Their staff members watch them closely, and if they see professionalism and optimism, they are likely to demonstrate those characteristics as well. Preach the gospel of conscious comportment—a constant awareness of the image one is projecting to the world. If you observe a manager projecting a less-than-positive image, tell that person right away.

You should also be alert to new managers who undermine their own authority. Linda made another classic rookie mistake when she attempted to get her staff members to implement an initiative that her boss had come up with. In presenting the initiative, she let her team know it was important to implement because it had come from the division's senior vice president. While her intentions were good—rallying the team to perform—her words encouraged the group to focus attention above her rather than on her. There is no quicker way for a rookie manager to lose credibility with her staff than to appear to be a mouthpiece for senior management. Pointing out that senior management will be checking up on the initiative certainly won't hurt, but the rookie manager must take care never to be perceived simply as the messenger.

Just-in-time coaching is often the most effective method for showing rookie managers how to project confidence. For instance, the first time you ask a new manager to carry out an initiative, take a little extra time to walk her through the process. Impress upon her the cardinal rule of management: Your staff members don't necessarily have to like you, but they do need to trust you. Ensure that the new manager owns the message she's delivering.

Layoffs are a classic example of a message the rookie manager will struggle with. Don't allow a rookie to proceed half-prepared. Share as much information as you can. Make sure she's ready for all the likely questions and reactions by asking her to do an informal dry run with you. You might be surprised by how poorly she conveys the message in her first few attempts. A little practice may preserve the image of your manager and your company.

Focusing on the Big Picture

Rookie managers have a real knack for allowing immediate tasks to overshadow overarching initiatives. This is particularly true for those promoted from within, because they've just come from the front lines where they're accustomed to constant fire fighting. As a recent individual contributor armed with plenty of technical know-how, the rookie manager instinctively runs to the immediate rescue of any client or staff member in need. The sense of accomplishment rookies get from such rescues is seductive and far more exhilarating than rooting out the cause of all the fire fighting. And what could be better for team spirit than having the boss jump into the trenches and fight the good fight?

Of course, a leader shows great team spirit if he joins the troops in emergencies. But are all those emergencies true emergencies? Are newer staff members being empowered to handle complex challenges? And if the rookie manager is busy fighting fires, who is thinking strategically for the department? If you're the senior manager and these questions are popping into your head, you may well have a rookie manager who doesn't fully understand his role or is afraid to seize it.

I recently worked with a young manager who had become so accustomed to responding to a steady flow of problems that he was reluctant to block off any time to work on the strategic initiatives we had identified. When I probed, he revealed that he felt a critical part of his role was to wait for crises to arise. "What if I schedule this time and something urgent comes up and I disappoint someone?" he asked. When I pointed out that he could always postpone his strategy sessions if a true emergency arose, he seemed relieved. But he saw the concept of making time to think about the business as self-indulgent—this, despite the fact that his group was going to be asked to raise productivity significantly in the following fiscal year, and he'd done nothing to prepare for that reality.

Senior managers can help rookies by explaining to them that strategic thinking is a necessary skill for career advancement: For first-time managers, 10% of the work might be strategic and 90% tactical. As executives climb the corporate ladder, however, those percentages will flip-flop. To be successful at the next level, managers must demonstrate that they can think and act strategically. You can use your regularly scheduled meetings to help your managers focus on the big picture. Don't allow them to simply review the latest results and move on. Ask probing questions about those results. For example, "What trends are you seeing in the marketplace that could affect you in two quarters? Tell me how your competition is responding to those same trends." Don't let them regale you with the wonderful training their staffs have been getting without asking, "What additional skills do we need to build in the staff to increase productivity by 25% next year?" If you aren't satisfied with your managers' responses, let them know that you expect them to think this way—not to have all the answers, but to be fully engaged in the strategic thought process.

Rookie managers commonly focus on activities rather than on goals. That's because activities can be accomplished quickly (for example, conducting a seminar to improve the sales staff's presentation skills), whereas achieving goals generally takes more time (for example, actually enhancing the sales staff's effectiveness). The senior manager can help the rookie manager think strategically by asking for written goals that clearly distinguish between the goals and their supporting activities. Insisting on a goal-setting discipline will help your new (and not-so-new) managers to organize their strategic game plans. Critical but soft goals, such as staff development, are often overlooked because they are difficult to measure. Putting such goals in print with clear action steps makes them concrete, rendering a sense of accomplishment when they are achieved and a greater likelihood that they will be rewarded. Managers with clear goals will be less tempted to become full-time tacticians. Just as important, the process will help you ensure that they are thinking about the right issues and deploying their teams effectively.

Giving Constructive Feedback

It's human nature to avoid confrontations, and most people feel awkward when they have to correct others' behavior or actions. Rookie managers are no exception, and they often avoid addressing important issues with their staff. The typical scenario goes something like this: A staff member is struggling to meet performance goals or is acting inappropriately in meetings. The manager sits back, watches, and hopes that things will magically improve. Other staff members observe the situation and become frustrated by the manager's inaction. The manager's own frustration builds, as she can't believe the subordinate doesn't get it. The straightforward performance issue has now evolved into a credibility problem. When the manager finally addresses the problem, she personalizes it, lets her frustration seep into the discussion with her staff member, and finds the recipient rushing to defend himself from attack.

Most inexperienced managers wait far too long to talk with staff about performance problems. The senior manager can help by creating an environment in which constructive feedback is perceived not as criticism but as a source of empowerment. This begins with the feedback you offer to your managers about their own development. It can be as simple as getting them to tell you where their weaknesses are before they become problematic. After a good performance review, for example, you might say to your new manager, "By all accounts, you have a bright future here, so it's important that we talk about what you *don't* want me to know. What are you feeling least confident about? How can we address those areas so that you're ready for any opportunity that arises?" You'll probably be surprised by how attuned most high performers are to their own development needs. But they are not likely to do much about them unless you put those needs on the table.

More than likely, the feedback your managers have to offer their staffs will not always be so positive or easy to deliver. The key is to foster in them the desire to help their reports achieve their goals. Under those circumstances, even loathsome personal issues become approachable.

One of my clients managed a high-performing senior staff member who was notably unhelpful to others in the department and who resented her own lack of advancement. Instead of avoiding the issue because he didn't want to tell the staff member that she had a bad attitude, the senior manager took a more productive approach. He leveraged his knowledge of her personal goals to introduce the feedback. "I know that you're anxious for your first management role, and one of my goals is to help you attain that. I can't do that unless I'm completely honest with you. A big part of management is developing stronger skills in your staff. You aren't demonstrating that you enjoy that role. How can we can work together on that?" No guilt, no admonishment—just an offer to help her get what she wanted. Yet the message was received loud and clear.

A brainstorming session this client and I had about ways to offer critical feedback led to that approach. Often, brainstorming sessions can help rookie managers see that sticky personal issues can be broken down into straightforward business issues. In the case of the unhelpful senior staff member, her attitude didn't really need to enter the discussion; her actions did. Recommending a change in action is much easier than recommending a change in attitude. Never forget the old saw: You can't ask people to change their personalities, but you can ask them to change their behaviors.

Indeed, senior managers should share their own techniques for dealing with difficult conversations. One manager I worked with became defensive whenever a staff member questioned her judgment. She didn't really need me to tell her that her behavior was undermining her image and effectiveness. She did need me to offer her some techniques that would enable her to respond differently in the heat of the moment. She trained herself to respond quickly and earnestly with a small repertoire of questions like, "Can you tell me more about what you mean by that?" This simple technique bought her the time she needed to gather her thoughts and engage in an interchange that was productive rather than defensive. She was too close to the situation to come up with the technique herself.

Delegating, thinking strategically, communicating—you may think this all sounds like Management 101. And you're right. The most basic elements of management are often what trip up managers early in their careers. And because they are the basics, the bosses of rookie managers often take them for granted. They shouldn't—an extraordinary number of people fail to develop these skills. I've maintained an illusion throughout this article—that only rookie managers suffer because they haven't mastered these core skills. But the truth is, managers at all levels make these mistakes. An organization that supports its new managers by helping them to develop these skills will have surprising advantages over the competition.

Originally published in April 2002. Reprint R0204H

Managing the High-Intensity Workplace

by Erin Reid and Lakshmi Ramarajan

TALES OF TIME-HUNGRY ORGANIZATIONS—from Silicon Valley to Wall Street and from London to Hong Kong—abound. Managers routinely overload their subordinates, contact them outside of business hours, and make last-minute requests for additional work. To satisfy those demands, employees arrive early, stay late, pull all-nighters, work weekends, and remain tied to their electronic devices 24/7. And those who are unable—or unwilling—to respond typically get penalized.

By operating in this way, organizations pressure employees to become what sociologists have called ideal workers: people totally dedicated to their jobs and always on call. The phenomenon is widespread in professional and managerial settings; it's been documented in depth at tech start-ups, at investment banks, and in medical organizations. In such places, any suggestion of meaningful outside interests and commitments can signal a lack of fitness for the job.

That's what Carla Harris feared when she started at Morgan Stanley, where she is now a senior executive. She also happens to be a passionate gospel singer with three CDs and numerous concerts to her credit. But early in her business career, she kept that part of her life private, concerned that being open about the time she devoted to singing would hurt her professionally. Multiple research studies suggest that she had good reason to worry.

To be ideal workers, people must choose, again and again, to prioritize their jobs ahead of other parts of their lives: their role as parents (actual or anticipated), their personal needs, and even their health. This reality is difficult to talk about, let alone challenge, because despite the well-documented personal and physical costs of these choices, an overwhelming number of people believe that achieving success *requires* them and those around them to conform to this ideal. That commonplace belief sometimes even causes people to resist well-planned organizational changes that could reduce the pressure to be available day and night. When Best Buy, for example, attempted to focus on results and avoid long work hours, some managers balked, holding tightly to the belief that selfless devotion to the job was necessary.

The pressure to be an ideal worker is well established, but how people cope with it—and with what consequences—is too often left unexplored. Is it beneficial to weave ideal-worker expectations into a company culture? Is it necessary, at an individual level, to meet those expectations? Interviews that we have conducted with hundreds of professionals in a variety of fields—including consulting, finance, architecture, entrepreneurship, journalism, and teaching—suggest that being an ideal worker is often neither necessary nor beneficial. A majority of employees—men and women, parents and nonparents— find it difficult to stifle other aspects of themselves and focus single-mindedly on work. They grapple painfully with how to manage other parts of their lives. The solutions they arrive at may allow them to navigate the stresses, but they often suffer serious and dysfunctional consequences.

In the following pages, we describe strategies that people commonly use to manage the pressure to be 100% available and 100% committed to work, as well as the effects of those strategies on the individuals themselves, on those they supervise, and on the organizations they work for. Finally, we suggest a route to a healthier—and ultimately more productive—organizational culture that can be driven by individual managers' small changes.

Idea in Brief

The Context

The expectation that people will be totally available and committed to work has never been stronger—but even in high-intensity environments, most people don't conform to that ideal.

The Problem

The strategies employees use to cope with unrealistic expectations

often prove damaging to them and to the organizations they work for.

The Solution

It's time to redefine the "ideal" worker. People will be more engaged and productive—and organizations more successful—if individuals aren't pressured to suppress their complicated, multilayered identities.

Three Strategies

In our research we found that people typically rely on one of three strategies: *accepting* and conforming to the demands of a high-pressure workplace; *passing* as ideal workers by quietly finding ways around the norm; or *revealing* their other commitments and their unwillingness to abandon them.

Accepting

Many people manage the pressure to be fully devoted to work by simply giving in and conforming. Indeed, at one consulting firm among the companies we studied, 43% of the people interviewed fell into this group. In their quest to succeed on the job, "accepters" prioritize their work identities and sacrifice or significantly suppress other meaningful aspects of who they are. People we spoke to across professions told us, somewhat ruefully, of giving up dreams of being civically engaged, running marathons, or getting deeply involved in their family lives. One architect reported:

> For me, design is 24/7. This project I'm designing, my boss e-mails me at all hours of the night—midnight, 6 AM. I can never plan my time, and I'm kind of at his beck and call.

When work is enjoyable and rewarding, an accepting strategy may be beneficial, allowing people to succeed and advance in their careers. But a professional identity that crowds out everything else makes people more vulnerable to career threats, because they have psychologically put all their eggs in one basket. When job loss or other setbacks occur, accepters find it particularly difficult to cope, as other parts of their lives have withered away. For accepters, treating work as the be-all and end-all may be fulfilling when the job is going well, but it leads to fragility in the long term.

Furthermore, people who buy in to the ideal-worker culture find it difficult to understand those who do not. As a result, accepters can become the main drivers of organizational pressure for round-the-clock availability. They tend to have trouble managing people who have lives outside the office. One senior consultant, describing the kind of employee he prefers to work with, said:

> I want someone who's lying awake at night thinking, Man, what are we going to do in this meeting tomorrow? Because that's what I do.

Perhaps surprisingly, accepters aren't necessarily good mentors even to people who are trying to conform to the organization's expectations. It can be difficult for junior colleagues to get these individuals' time and attention, in part because accepters are so absorbed in the job. In the words of one consultant, "They can no longer understand how unbelievably stressful it is to come in not knowing how to play the game." As a result, they often take a sink-or-swim approach to junior-colleague development.

Passing
The strategy employed by another group of workers is to devote time to nonwork activities—but under the organization's radar. At the consulting firm, 27% of the study participants fell into this group. These people were "passing"—a term originally used by sociologist Erving Goffman to describe how people try to hide per-

sonal characteristics (such as physical disabilities or race) that might stigmatize them and subject them to discrimination. Consultants who were successful in passing as ideal workers received performance ratings that were just as high as those given to peers who genuinely embraced the 24/7 culture, and colleagues perceived them as being "always on."

We found that although people across professions developed ways to pass, their strategies for doing so varied. For example, some consultants focused on local industries, which permitted them to develop rosters of clients they could serve with minimal travel time, thus opening up space for other parts of their lives. One consultant explained how he was able to carve out time to sustain his romantic partnership and be an amateur athlete while still appearing to be an ideal worker:

> Travel comes out of your personal time, always. That's why I work for [local businesses]. They are all right nearby, and I take a car.

Another consultant also limited himself to working with local clients and often telecommuted to reduce his work hours. He used another key tool as well: controlling information about his whereabouts. He reported (with some pleasure) that he had actually skied every day the previous week—without claiming any personal time. Yet senior colleagues saw him as a rising star who worked much harder than most people at the firm.

For other passers, the ticket to success was not staying local but exploiting distance. A journalist we interviewed described taking a regional reporting assignment for a prestigious national newspaper, which allowed him to work from home, engage with his family, and file his articles in the evenings after his children went to bed, all while retaining a reputation as an ideal worker. He laughed, saying:

> No one ever really knew where I was, because I was hundreds of miles from the home base. I was the only one in my region.

Although passing enables people to survive in demanding cultures without giving their all to work, passers pay a psychological price for hiding parts of themselves from their colleagues, superiors, and subordinates. Human beings have a need to express themselves and to be known by others. When important aspects of their identities cannot be shared at work, people may feel insecure and inauthentic—not to mention disengaged. These feelings have real costs for organizations, too: Our research indicates that over time, passers have a relatively high turnover rate. This suggests that although they may get by in the short term, hiding key dimensions of themselves from their colleagues can be difficult to sustain in the long run.

Passing as an ideal worker can also make it hard to manage others. Passers don't necessarily want to encourage conformance to the ideal-worker image, but on the other hand, advising subordinates to pass—and effectively engage in subterfuge—is also problematic. So is suggesting open resistance to the demands for round-the clock availability, because (as we shall see) the careers of people who resist are likely to suffer. To complicate matters further, passers may believe that most people in the organization *want* to work all the time. One senior leader who himself passed but avoided counseling his employees to do likewise made this comment:

> I want [my employees] to be happy, but if they derive their happiness from working a lot, that's not for me to judge.

A subtly destructive aspect of passing is that by failing to openly challenge the ideal-worker culture, passers allow that culture to persist. Their track records prove that people don't need to be workaholics to succeed—but the organization continues to design and measure work as if that were the case.

Revealing

Not everyone wants to pass—or can—and some who initially pass grow frustrated with this strategy over time. These people cope by openly sharing other parts of their lives and by asking for changes to the structure of their work, such as reduced schedules and other formal accommodations. At the consulting firm, 30% of those interviewed pursued this strategy. Although it's often assumed that people who resist the pressure to be ideal workers are primarily women with families, we have not encountered enormous gender differences in our research. Data from the consulting firm shows that fewer than half of the women were "revealers," while more than a quarter of the men were.

Revealing allows people the validation of being more fully known by colleagues, which is denied to the passers. However, it can have damaging career consequences. At the consulting firm, performance reviews and promotion data showed that revealers paid a substantial penalty. For example, one consultant indicated his unwillingness to make work his top priority when he asked for paternity leave. With his wife eight months pregnant, the soon-to-be father expected a temporary reprieve. Instead, he faced questions about his dedication:

> One of the partners said to me, "You have a choice to make. Are you going to be a professional, or are you going to be just an average person in your field? If you are going to be a professional, then nothing else can be as important to you as your work. If you want to be world-class, it's got to be all-consuming."

Over time, being sanctioned for failure to conform can lead to resentment. Instead of motivating people to devote themselves first and foremost to their work, it may cause them to leave the organization in search of a better fit.

The experience of revealing their nonwork commitments and being penalized for doing so can make it difficult for people to manage others. Like passers, revealers may struggle with encouraging their subordinates to accept ideal-worker pressures, but they may shy away from advising resistance because they know the costs firsthand.

Surviving a High-Intensity Workplace

THERE'S NO PERFECT STRATEGY for managing oneself in an organization that values selfless dedication, but it's useful to know your own tendencies, understand their risks, and mitigate those risks to the extent possible. To get started, think about **how you tend to respond to e-mails by colleagues in the evenings** and read the table on the next page.

There Has to Be a Better Way

Our research suggests that if employees felt free to draw some lines between their professional and personal lives, organizations would benefit from greater engagement, more-open relationships, and more paths to success. We outline three steps that managers can take to create a richer definition of what it means to be an "ideal" worker—without sacrificing high performance. These changes don't have to be pushed by a senior leader within the organization; they can be effectively implemented at the team level.

Develop your own multifaceted identity

People in leadership positions can avoid the fragility that results from blind acceptance of ideal-worker norms by deliberately cultivating their own nonwork identities: a civic self, an athletic self, a family-oriented self. One architect told us that when he defined himself solely in terms of his work, professional struggles and setbacks made him miserable. Ironically, as he broadened his focus, he found more professional fulfillment. As managers become more resilient, they may also learn that employees whose lives are better balanced create value for the organization.

Managers can start to change organizational norms by pointing out the positive things that employees' outside activities bring to the workplace. One consultant whose firm had recently merged with another enterprise observed that none of his new colleagues ever stayed in the office past 5:30 PM. When he asked about this pattern, he was told:

> We don't want our folks to spend every waking minute at work; we want them to be well-rounded individuals, to be curious, to

Response	Strategy	Motivation	Risks to be aware of	What you can alter
RAPID ENGAGEMENT. You always reply and, if requested, bang out some work (e.g., "I'll have it for you in five minutes!"). You rarely make evening plans.	ACCEPTING	You devote yourself completely to work because it is expected and rewarded.	You may burn out or be slow to rebound from setbacks. You may have trouble mentoring others and creating a pipeline of promotable employees.	Set aside blocks of time for other aspects of your life. Don't expect subordinates to make work their highest priority. Be open to different ways of working.
FEIGNED ATTENTIVENESS. You respond and give the impression that you are working (e.g., "Am on it—will take a few hours"). You tend to make and keep evening plans but rarely mention them.	PASSING	You seek to protect your career while sustaining other aspects of your life.	You may not build close relationships at work. You may perpetuate the ideal-worker myth.	Come out to selected colleagues so you feel better known and they don't feel compelled to sacrifice their personal lives. Make it clear that outside activities don't hurt your performance.
NEXT-DAY FOLLOW-UP. Unless it's urgent, you don't alter your plans (e.g., "At a show—will get to this tomorrow"). You may not even respond that evening.	REVEALING	You wish to be open in your relationships and believe the organization may need to change.	You may damage your career. You may sacrifice the credibility needed to push for change.	Emphasize results, not effort, when discussing work. Encourage others to be open about their behavior and thus change workplace norms.

see things out in the world, and to have all kinds of different experiences that they can then bring to bear on their work.

People who pursue outside activities—volunteering in local politics, for example, or at a child's school—are exposed to experiences, specialized knowledge, and networks that would be unavailable to them if they had spent that time holed up at the office.

Minimize time-based rewards

Employees who choose a passing strategy do so in part because it's common to evaluate *how much* people work (or seem to), rather than the quality of their output. This tendency is often reinforced by subtle and not-so-subtle beliefs and practices. For example, a senior consultant expressed his conviction that successful consultants must have the "high-five factor": They've spent so much time on-site with the client that when they enter the client's building, employees give them high fives. One firm we worked with awarded a prize to the person who had taken the most flights in a year. Valuing work time over work product—which motivates people to deceive others about how many hours they're clocking—is an easy trap to fall into, especially for professionals, whose knowledge-based work is difficult to evaluate.

We propose that managers reduce the incentives for passing (and the costs of revealing) by encouraging people to focus on achieving their goals and measuring actual results rather than hours invested. For example, instead of celebrating a high-five factor based on time spent with the client, managers could praise employees for the quality of the advice provided or the number of repeat engagements secured. Managers can also move away from time-based rewards by working to set reasonable expectations with clients.

Other policy changes can be made even more easily. One employee we interviewed remarked that her current boss differed from her old one because he believed late nights were a sign that she was working inefficiently, and he discouraged them. Another employee stated that her manager simply asked her to set her own deadlines—realistically. When given such autonomy, high-performing workers who would otherwise pass or reveal are likely to follow through on their commitments.

Protect employees' personal lives

Most organizations leave it to their employees to set boundaries between their work and their nonwork lives—often with the best intentions. When Netflix offered unlimited time off, for example, managers thought they were treating their people like "grown-ups." But providing complete freedom can heighten employees' fears that their choices will signal a lack of commitment. Without clear direction, many employees simply default to the ideal-worker expectation, suppressing the need to live more-balanced lives.

Managers have the power to change this by flipping the script and actively protecting employees' nonwork time and identities. They can, for example, institute required vacations, regular leaves, and reasonable work hours—for all employees, not just some. Making a firm commitment to avoid excessive workloads and extreme and unpredictable hours, rather than simply giving people the option to request downtime, will help them engage with other parts of their selves.

THE PRESSURE to be an ideal worker is at an all-time high, but so are the costs to both individuals and their employers. Moreover, the experiences of those who are able to pass as ideal workers suggest that superhuman dedication may not always be necessary for organizational success. By valuing all aspects of people's identities, rewarding work output instead of work time, and taking steps to protect employees' personal lives, leaders can begin to unravel the ideal-worker myth that has become woven into the fabric of their organizations. And that will enhance employees' resilience, their creativity, and their satisfaction on the job.

Originally published in June 2016. Reprint R1606G

Harnessing the Science of Persuasion

by Robert B. Cialdini

A LUCKY FEW HAVE IT; MOST of us do not. A handful of gifted "naturals" simply know how to capture an audience, sway the undecided, and convert the opposition. Watching these masters of persuasion work their magic is at once impressive and frustrating. What's impressive is not just the easy way they use charisma and eloquence to convince others to do as they ask. It's also how eager those others are to do what's requested of them, as if the persuasion itself were a favor they couldn't wait to repay.

The frustrating part of the experience is that these born persuaders are often unable to account for their remarkable skill or pass it on to others. Their way with people is an art, and artists as a rule are far better at doing than at explaining. Most of them can't offer much help to those of us who possess no more than the ordinary quotient of charisma and eloquence but who still have to wrestle with leadership's fundamental challenge: getting things done through others. That challenge is painfully familiar to corporate executives, who every day have to figure out how to motivate and direct a highly individualistic work force. Playing the "Because I'm the boss" card is out. Even if it weren't demeaning and demoralizing for all concerned, it would be out of place in a world where cross-functional teams, joint ventures, and intercompany partnerships have blurred the lines of authority. In such an environment, persuasion skills exert far greater influence over others' behavior than formal power structures do.

Which brings us back to where we started. Persuasion skills may be more necessary than ever, but how can executives acquire them if the most talented practitioners can't pass them along? By looking to science. For the past five decades, behavioral scientists have conducted experiments that shed considerable light on the way certain interactions lead people to concede, comply, or change. This research shows that persuasion works by appealing to a limited set of deeply rooted human drives and needs, and it does so in predictable ways. Persuasion, in other words, is governed by basic principles that can be taught, learned, and applied. By mastering these principles, executives can bring scientific rigor to the business of securing consensus, cutting deals, and winning concessions. In the pages that follow, I describe six fundamental principles of persuasion and suggest a few ways that executives can apply them in their own organizations.

The Principle of Liking

People like those who like them.

The application
Uncover real similarities and offer genuine praise.

The retailing phenomenon known as the Tupperware party is a vivid illustration of this principle in action. The demonstration party for Tupperware products is hosted by an individual, almost always a woman, who invites to her home an array of friends, neighbors, and relatives. The guests' affection for their hostess predisposes them to buy from her, a dynamic that was confirmed by a 1990 study of purchase decisions made at demonstration parties. The researchers, Jonathan Frenzen and Harry Davis, writing in the *Journal of Consumer Research*, found that the guests' fondness for their hostess weighed twice as heavily in their purchase decisions as their regard for the products they bought. So when guests at a Tupperware party

Idea in Brief

If leadership, at its most basic, consists of getting things done through others, then persuasion is one of the leader's essential tools. Many executives have assumed that this tool is beyond their grasp, available only to the charismatic and the eloquent. Over the past several decades, though, experimental psychologists have learned which methods reliably lead people to concede, comply, or change. Their research shows that persuasion is governed by several principles that can be taught and applied. The first principle is that people are more likely to follow someone who is similar to them than someone who is not. Wise managers, then, enlist peers to help make their cases. Second, people are more willing to cooperate with those who are not only like them but who like them, as well. So it's worth the time to uncover real similarities and offer genuine praise. Third, experiments confirm the intuitive truth that people tend to treat you the way you treat them. It's sound policy to do a favor before seeking one. Fourth, individuals are more likely to keep promises they make voluntarily and explicitly. The message for managers here is to get commitments in writing. Fifth, studies show that people really do defer to experts. So before they attempt to exert influence, executives should take pains to establish their own expertise and not assume that it's self-evident. Finally, people want more of a commodity when it's scarce; it follows, then, that exclusive information is more persuasive than widely available data. By mastering these principles—and, the author stresses, using them judiciously and ethically—executives can learn the elusive art of capturing an audience, swaying the undecided, and converting the opposition.

buy something, they aren't just buying to please themselves. They're buying to please their hostess as well.

What's true at Tupperware parties is true for business in general: If you want to influence people, win friends. How? Controlled research has identified several factors that reliably increase liking, but two stand out as especially compelling—similarity and praise. Similarity literally draws people together. In one experiment, reported in a 1968 article in the *Journal of Personality*, participants stood physically closer to one another after learning that they shared political beliefs and social values. And in a 1963 article in *American Behavioral Scientists*, researcher F. B. Evans used demographic data

Idea in Practice

Persuasion Principles

Principle	Example	Business application
LIKING: People like those like them, who like them.	At Tupperware parties, guests' fondness for their host influences purchase decisions twice as much as regard for the products.	**To influence people, win friends,** through: *Similarity*: Create *early* bonds with new peers, bosses, and direct reports by informally discovering common interests—you'll establish goodwill and trustworthiness. *Praise*: Charm *and* disarm. Make positive remarks about others—you'll generate more willing compliance.
RECIPROCITY: People repay in kind.	When the Disabled American Veterans enclosed free personalized address labels in donation-request envelops, response rate doubled.	**Give what you want to receive.** Lend a staff member to a colleague who needs help; you'll get *his* help later.
SOCIAL PROOF: People follow the lead of similar others.	More New York City residents tried returning a lost wallet after learning that other New Yorkers had tried.	**Use peer power** to influence horizontally, not vertically; e.g., ask an esteemed "old timer" to support your new initiative if other veterans resist.

from insurance company records to demonstrate that prospects were more willing to purchase a policy from a salesperson who was akin to them in age, religion, politics, or even cigarette-smoking habits.

Managers can use similarities to create bonds with a recent hire, the head of another department, or even a new boss. Informal conversations during the workday create an ideal opportunity to discover at least one common area of enjoyment, be it a hobby, a college basketball team, or reruns of *Seinfeld*. The important thing is to establish the bond early because it creates a presumption of goodwill and trustworthiness in every subsequent encounter. It's much easier to build support for a new project when the people you're trying to persuade are already inclined in your favor.

Principle	Example	Business application
CONSISTENCY: People fulfill written, public, and voluntary commitments.	92% of residents of an apartment complex who signed a petition supporting a new recreation center later donated money to the cause.	**Make others' commitments active, public, and voluntary.** If you supervise an employee who should submit reports on time, get that understanding in writing (a memo); make the commitment public (note colleagues' agreement with the memo); and link the commitment to the employee's values (the impact of timely reports on team spirit).
AUTHORITY: People defer to experts who provide short-cuts to decisions requiring specialized information.	A single *New York Times* expert opinion news story aired on TV generates a 4% shift in U.S. public opinion.	**Don't assume your expertise is self-evident.** Instead, establish your expertise *before* doing business with new colleagues or partners; e.g., in conversations before an important meeting, describe how you solved a problem similar to the one on the agenda.
SCARCITY: People value what's scarce.	Wholesale beef buyers' orders jumped 600% when they alone received information on a possible beef shortage.	**Use exclusive information to persuade.** Influence and rivet key players' attention by saying, for example: ". . . Just got this information today. It won't be distributed until next week."

Praise, the other reliable generator of affection, both charms and disarms. Sometimes the praise doesn't even have to be merited. Researchers at the University of North Carolina writing in the *Journal of Experimental Social Psychology* found that men felt the greatest regard for an individual who flattered them unstintingly even if the comments were untrue. And in their book *Interpersonal Attraction* (Addison-Wesley, 1978), Ellen Berscheid and Elaine Hatfield Walster presented experimental data showing that positive remarks about another person's traits, attitude, or performance reliably generates liking in return, as well as willing compliance with the wishes of the person offering the praise.

Along with cultivating a fruitful relationship, adroit managers can also use praise to repair one that's damaged or unproductive.

65

Imagine you're the manager of a good-sized unit within your organization. Your work frequently brings you into contact with another manager—call him Dan—whom you have come to dislike. No matter how much you do for him, it's not enough. Worse, he never seems to believe that you're doing the best you can for him. Resenting his attitude and his obvious lack of trust in your abilities and in your good faith, you don't spend as much time with him as you know you should; in consequence, the performance of both his unit and yours is deteriorating.

The research on praise points toward a strategy for fixing the relationship. It may be hard to find, but there has to be something about Dan you can sincerely admire, whether it's his concern for the people in his department, his devotion to his family, or simply his work ethic. In your next encounter with him, make an appreciative comment about that trait. Make it clear that in this case at least, you value what he values. I predict that Dan will relax his relentless negativity and give you an opening to convince him of your competence and good intentions.

The Principle of Reciprocity

People repay in kind.

The application
Give what you want to receive.

Praise is likely to have a warming and softening effect on Dan because, ornery as he is, he is still human and subject to the universal human tendency to treat people the way they treat him. If you have ever caught yourself smiling at a coworker just because he or she smiled first, you know how this principle works.

Charities rely on reciprocity to help them raise funds. For years, for instance, the Disabled American Veterans organization, using only a well-crafted fund-raising letter, garnered a very respectable 18% rate of response to its appeals. But when the group started enclosing a small gift in the envelope, the response rate nearly doubled to 35%. The gift—personalized address labels—was extremely modest, but it wasn't what prospective donors received that made the difference. It was that they had gotten anything at all.

What works in that letter works at the office, too. It's more than an effusion of seasonal spirit, of course, that impels suppliers to shower gifts on purchasing departments at holiday time. In 1996, purchasing managers admitted to an interviewer from *Inc.* magazine that after having accepted a gift from a supplier, they were willing to purchase products and services they would have otherwise declined. Gifts also have a startling effect on retention. I have encouraged readers of my book to send me examples of the principles of influence at work in their own lives. One reader, an employee of the State of Oregon, sent a letter in which she offered these reasons for her commitment to her supervisor:

> He gives me and my son gifts for Christmas and gives me presents on my birthday. There is no promotion for the type of job I have, and my only choice for one is to move to another department. But I find myself resisting trying to move. My boss is reaching retirement age, and I am thinking I will be able to move out after he retires. . . . [F]or now, I feel obligated to stay since he has been so nice to me.

Ultimately, though, gift giving is one of the cruder applications of the rule of reciprocity. In its more sophisticated uses, it confers a genuine first-mover advantage on any manager who is trying to foster positive attitudes and productive personal relationships in the office: Managers can elicit the desired behavior from coworkers and employees by displaying it first. Whether it's a sense of trust, a spirit of cooperation, or a pleasant demeanor, leaders should model the behavior they want to see from others.

The same holds true for managers faced with issues of information delivery and resource allocation. If you lend a member of your staff to a colleague who is shorthanded and staring at a fast-approaching deadline, you will significantly increase your chances of getting help when you need it. Your odds will improve even more if you say, when your colleague thanks you for the assistance, something like, "Sure, glad to help. I know how important it is for me to count on your help when I need it."

The Principle of Social Proof

People follow the lead of similar others.

The application

Use peer power whenever it's available.

Social creatures that they are, human beings rely heavily on the people around them for cues on how to think, feel, and act. We know this intuitively, but intuition has also been confirmed by experiments, such as the one first described in 1982 in the *Journal of Applied Psychology*. A group of researchers went door-to-door in Columbia, South Carolina, soliciting donations for a charity campaign and displaying a list of neighborhood residents who had already donated to the cause. The researchers found that the longer the donor list was, the more likely those solicited would be to donate as well.

To the people being solicited, the friends' and neighbors' names on the list were a form of social evidence about how they should respond. But the evidence would not have been nearly as compelling had the names been those of random strangers. In an experiment from the 1960s, first described in the *Journal of Personality and Social Psychology*, residents of New York City were asked to return a lost wallet to its owner. They were highly likely to attempt to return the wallet when they learned that another New Yorker had previously attempted to do so. But learning that someone from a foreign country had tried to return the wallet didn't sway their decision one way or the other.

The lesson for executives from these two experiments is that persuasion can be extremely effective when it comes from peers. The science supports what most sales professionals already know: Testimonials from satisfied customers work best when the satisfied customer and the prospective customer share similar circumstances. That lesson can help a manager faced with the task of selling a new corporate initiative. Imagine that you're trying to streamline your department's work processes. A group of veteran employees is resisting. Rather than try to convince the employees of the move's merits yourself, ask an old-timer who supports the initiative to speak up for it at a team meeting. The compatriot's testimony stands a much better chance of convincing the group than yet another speech from the boss. Stated simply, influence is often best exerted horizontally rather than vertically.

The Principle of Consistency

People align with their clear commitments.

The application
Make their commitments active, public, and voluntary.

Liking is a powerful force, but the work of persuasion involves more than simply making people feel warmly toward you, your idea, or your product. People need not only to like you but to feel committed to what you want them to do. Good turns are one reliable way to make people feel obligated to you. Another is to win a public commitment from them.

My own research has demonstrated that most people, once they take a stand or go on record in favor of a position, prefer to stick to it. Other studies reinforce that finding and go on to show how even a small, seemingly trivial commitment can have a powerful effect on future actions. Israeli researchers writing in 1983 in the *Personality and Social Psychology Bulletin* recounted how they asked half the residents of a large apartment complex to sign a petition favoring the establishment of a recreation center for the handicapped. The cause was good and the request was small, so almost everyone who was asked agreed to sign. Two weeks later, on National Collection Day for the Handicapped, all residents of the complex were approached at home and asked to give to the cause. A little more than half of those who were not asked to sign the petition made a contribution. But an astounding 92% of those who did sign donated money. The residents of the apartment complex felt obligated to live up to their commitments because those commitments were active, public, and voluntary. These three features are worth considering separately.

There's strong empirical evidence to show that a choice made actively—one that's spoken out loud or written down or otherwise made explicit—is considerably more likely to direct someone's future conduct than the same choice left unspoken. Writing in 1996 in the *Personality and Social Psychology Bulletin*, Delia Cioffi and Randy Garner described an experiment in which college students in one group were asked to fill out a printed form saying they wished to volunteer for an AIDS education project in the public schools. Students in another group volunteered for the same project by leaving blank a form stating that they didn't want to participate. A few days later, when the volunteers reported for duty, 74% of those who showed up were students from the group that signaled their commitment by filling out the form.

The implications are clear for a manager who wants to persuade a subordinate to follow some particular course of action: Get it in writing. Let's suppose you want your employee to submit reports in a more timely fashion. Once you believe you've won agreement, ask him to summarize the decision in a memo and send it to you. By doing so, you'll have greatly increased the odds that he'll fulfill the commitment because, as a rule, people live up to what they have written down.

Research into the social dimensions of commitment suggests that written statements become even more powerful when they're made public. In a classic experiment, described in 1955 in the *Journal of Abnormal and Social Psychology*, college students were asked to estimate the length of lines projected on a screen. Some students were asked to write down their choices on a piece of paper, sign it, and hand the paper to the experimenter. Others wrote their choices on an erasable slate, then erased the slate immediately. Still others were instructed to keep their decisions to themselves.

The experimenters then presented all three groups with evidence that their initial choices may have been wrong. Those who had merely kept their decisions in their heads were the most likely to reconsider their original estimates. More loyal to their first guesses were the students in the group that had written them down and immediately erased them. But by a wide margin, the ones most reluctant to shift from their original choices were those who had signed and handed them to the researcher.

This experiment highlights how much most people wish to appear consistent to others. Consider again the matter of the employee who has been submitting late reports. Recognizing the power of this desire, you should, once you've successfully convinced him of the need to be more timely, reinforce the commitment by making sure it gets a public airing. One way to do that would be to send the employee an e-mail that reads, "I think your plan is just what we need. I showed it to Diane in manufacturing and Phil in shipping, and they thought it was right on target, too." Whatever way such commitments are formalized, they should never be like the New Year's resolutions people privately make and then abandon with no one the wiser. They should be publicly made and visibly posted.

More than 300 years ago, Samuel Butler wrote a couplet that explains succinctly why commitments must be voluntary to be lasting and effective: "He that complies against his will/Is of his own opinion still." If an undertaking is forced, coerced, or imposed from the outside, it's not a commitment; it's an unwelcome burden. Think how you would react if your boss pressured you to donate to the campaign of a political candidate. Would that make you more apt to opt for that candidate in the privacy of a voting booth? Not likely. In fact, in their 1981 book *Psychological Reactance* (Academic Press), Sharon S. Brehm and Jack W. Brehm present data that suggest you'd vote the opposite way just to express your resentment of the boss's coercion.

This kind of backlash can occur in the office, too. Let's return again to that tardy employee. If you want to produce an enduring change in his behavior, you should avoid using threats or pressure tactics to gain his compliance. He'd likely view any change in his

Persuasion Experts, Safe at Last

THANKS TO SEVERAL DECADES OF rigorous empirical research by behavioral scientists, our understanding of the how and why of persuasion has never been broader, deeper, or more detailed. But these scientists aren't the first students of the subject. The history of persuasion studies is an ancient and honorable one, and it has generated a long roster of heroes and martyrs.

A renowned student of social influence, William McGuire, contends in a chapter of the *Handbook of Social Psychology*, 3rd ed. (Oxford University Press, 1985) that scattered among the more than four millennia of recorded Western history are four centuries in which the study of persuasion flourished as a craft. The first was the Periclean Age of ancient Athens, the second occurred during the years of the Roman Republic, the next appeared in the time of the European Renaissance, and the last extended over the hundred years that have just ended, which witnessed the advent of large-scale advertising, information, and mass media campaigns. Each of the three previous centuries of systematic persuasion study was marked by a flowering of human achievement that was suddenly cut short when political authorities had the masters

---

behavior as the result of intimidation rather than a personal commitment to change. A better approach would be to identify something that the employee genuinely values in the workplace—high-quality workmanship, perhaps, or team spirit—and then describe how timely reports are consistent with those values. That gives the employee reasons for improvement that he can own. And because he owns them, they'll continue to guide his behavior even when you're not watching.

The Principle of Authority

People defer to experts.

The application
Expose your expertise; don't assume it's self-evident.

Two thousand years ago, the Roman poet Virgil offered this simple counsel to those seeking to choose correctly: "Believe an expert." That

of persuasion killed. The philosopher Socrates is probably the best known of the persuasion experts to run afoul of the powers that be.

Information about the persuasion process is a threat because it creates a base of power entirely separate from the one controlled by political authorities. Faced with a rival source of influence, rulers in previous centuries had few qualms about eliminating those rare individuals who truly understood how to marshal forces that heads of state have never been able to monopolize, such as cleverly crafted language, strategically placed information, and, most important, psychological insight.

It would perhaps be expressing too much faith in human nature to claim that persuasion experts no longer face a threat from those who wield political power. But because the truth about persuasion is no longer the sole possession of a few brilliant, inspired individuals, experts in the field can presumably breathe a little easier. Indeed, since most people in power are interested in remaining in power, they're likely to be more interested in acquiring persuasion skills than abolishing them.

---

may or may not be good advice, but as a description of what people actually do, it can't be beaten. For instance, when the news media present an acknowledged expert's views on a topic, the effect on public opinion is dramatic. A single expert-opinion news story in the *New York Times* is associated with a 2% shift in public opinion nationwide, according to a 1993 study described in the *Public Opinion Quarterly*. And researchers writing in the *American Political Science Review* in 1987 found that when the expert's view was aired on national television, public opinion shifted as much as 4%. A cynic might argue that these findings only illustrate the docile submissiveness of the public. But a fairer explanation is that, amid the teeming complexity of contemporary life, a well-selected expert offers a valuable and efficient shortcut to good decisions. Indeed, some questions, be they legal, financial, medical, or technological, require so much specialized knowledge to answer, we have no choice but to rely on experts.

Since there's good reason to defer to experts, executives should take pains to ensure that they establish their own expertise before they attempt to exert influence. Surprisingly often, people mistakenly assume that others recognize and appreciate their experience. That's what happened at a hospital where some colleagues and I were consulting. The physical therapy staffers were frustrated because so many of their stroke patients abandoned their exercise routines as soon as they left the hospital. No matter how often the staff emphasized the importance of regular home exercise—it is, in fact, crucial to the process of regaining independent function—the message just didn't sink in.

Interviews with some of the patients helped us pinpoint the problem. They were familiar with the background and training of their physicians, but the patients knew little about the credentials of the physical therapists who were urging them to exercise. It was a simple matter to remedy that lack of information: We merely asked the therapy director to display all the awards, diplomas, and certifications of her staff on the walls of the therapy rooms. The result was startling: Exercise compliance jumped 34% and has never dropped since.

What we found immensely gratifying was not just how much we increased compliance, but how. We didn't fool or browbeat any of the patients. We *informed* them into compliance. Nothing had to be invented; no time or resources had to be spent in the process. The staff's expertise was real—all we had to do was make it more visible.

The task for managers who want to establish their claims to expertise is somewhat more difficult. They can't simply nail their diplomas to the wall and wait for everyone to notice. A little subtlety is called for. Outside the United States, it is customary for people to spend time interacting socially before getting down to business for the first time. Frequently they gather for dinner the night before their meeting or negotiation. These get-togethers can make discussions easier and help blunt disagreements—remember the findings about liking and similarity—and they can also provide an opportunity to establish expertise. Perhaps it's a matter of telling an anecdote about successfully solving a problem similar to the one that's on the agenda at the next day's meeting. Or perhaps dinner is the time to describe years spent mastering a complex discipline—not in a boastful way but as part of the ordinary give-and-take of conversation.

Granted, there's not always time for lengthy introductory sessions. But even in the course of the preliminary conversation that precedes most meetings, there is almost always an opportunity to touch lightly on your relevant background and experience as a natural part of a sociable exchange. This initial disclosure of personal information gives you a chance to establish expertise early in the game, so that when the discussion turns to the business at hand, what you have to say will be accorded the respect it deserves.

The Principle of Scarcity

People want more of what they can have less of.

The application
Highlight unique benefits and exclusive information.

Study after study shows that items and opportunities are seen to be more valuable as they become less available. That's a tremendously useful piece of information for managers. They can harness the scarcity principle with the organizational equivalents of limited-time, limited-supply, and one-of-a-kind offers. Honestly informing a coworker of a closing window of opportunity—the chance to get the boss's ear before she leaves for an extended vacation, perhaps—can mobilize action dramatically.

Managers can learn from retailers how to frame their offers not in terms of what people stand to gain but in terms of what they stand to lose if they don't act on the information. The power of "loss language" was demonstrated in a 1988 study of California home owners written up in the *Journal of Applied Psychology*. Half were told that if they fully insulated their homes, they would save a certain amount of money each day. The other half were told that if they failed to insulate, they would lose that amount each day. Significantly more people insulated their homes when exposed to the loss language. The same phenomenon occurs in business. According to a 1994 study in the journal *Organizational Behavior and Human Decision*

Processes, potential losses figure far more heavily in managers' decision making than potential gains.

In framing their offers, executives should also remember that exclusive information is more persuasive than widely available data. A doctoral student of mine, Amram Knishinsky, wrote his 1982 dissertation on the purchase decisions of wholesale beef buyers. He observed that they more than doubled their orders when they were told that, because of certain weather conditions overseas, there was likely to be a scarcity of foreign beef in the near future. But their orders increased 600% when they were informed that no one else had that information yet.

The persuasive power of exclusivity can be harnessed by any manager who comes into possession of information that's not broadly available and that supports an idea or initiative he or she would like the organization to adopt. The next time that kind of information crosses your desk, round up your organization's key players. The information itself may seem dull, but exclusivity will give it a special sheen. Push it across your desk and say, "I just got this report today. It won't be distributed until next week, but I want to give you an early look at what it shows." Then watch your listeners lean forward.

Allow me to stress here a point that should be obvious. No offer of exclusive information, no exhortation to act now or miss this opportunity forever should be made unless it is genuine. Deceiving colleagues into compliance is not only ethically objectionable, it's foolhardy. If the deception is detected—and it certainly will be—it will snuff out any enthusiasm the offer originally kindled. It will also invite dishonesty toward the deceiver. Remember the rule of reciprocity.

Putting It All Together

There's nothing abstruse or obscure about these six principles of persuasion. Indeed, they neatly codify our intuitive understanding of the ways people evaluate information and form decisions. As a result, the principles are easy for most people to grasp, even those with no formal education in psychology. But in the seminars and workshops I conduct, I have learned that two points bear repeated emphasis.

First, although the six principles and their applications can be discussed separately for the sake of clarity, they should be applied in combination to compound their impact. For instance, in discussing the importance of expertise, I suggested that managers use informal, social conversations to establish their credentials. But that conversation affords an opportunity to gain information as well as convey it. While you're showing your dinner companion that you have the skills and experience your business problem demands, you can also learn about your companion's background, likes, and dislikes—information that will help you locate genuine similarities and give sincere compliments. By letting your expertise surface and also establishing rapport, you double your persuasive power. And if you succeed in bringing your dinner partner on board, you may encourage other people to sign on as well, thanks to the persuasive power of social evidence.

The other point I wish to emphasize is that the rules of ethics apply to the science of social influence just as they do to any other technology. Not only is it ethically wrong to trick or trap others into assent, it's ill-advised in practical terms. Dishonest or high-pressure tactics work only in the short run, if at all. Their long-term effects are malignant, especially within an organization, which can't function properly without a bedrock level of trust and cooperation.

That point is made vividly in the following account, which a department head for a large textile manufacturer related at a training workshop I conducted. She described a vice president in her company who wrung public commitments from department heads in a highly manipulative manner. Instead of giving his subordinates time to talk or think through his proposals carefully, he would approach them individually at the busiest moment of their workday and describe the benefits of his plan in exhaustive, patience-straining detail. Then he would move in for the kill. "It's very important for me to see you as being on my team on this," he would say. "Can I count on your support?" Intimidated, frazzled, eager to chase the man from their offices so they could get back to work, the department heads would invariably go along with his request. But because the commitments never felt voluntary, the department heads never followed through, and as a result the vice president's initiatives all blew up or petered out.

This story had a deep impact on the other participants in the workshop. Some gulped in shock as they recognized their own manipulative behavior. But what stopped everyone cold was the expression on the department head's face as she recounted the damaging collapse of her superior's proposals. She was smiling.

Nothing I could say would more effectively make the point that the deceptive or coercive use of the principles of social influence is ethically wrong and pragmatically wrongheaded. Yet the same principles, if applied appropriately, can steer decisions correctly. Legitimate expertise, genuine obligations, authentic similarities, real social proof, exclusive news, and freely made commitments can produce choices that are likely to benefit both parties. And any approach that works to everyone's mutual benefit is good business, don't you think? Of course, I don't want to press you into it, but, if you agree, I would love it if you could just jot me a memo to that effect.

Originally published in September 2001. Reprint R0109D

What Makes a Leader?

by Daniel Goleman

EVERY BUSINESSPERSON KNOWS a story about a highly intelligent, highly skilled executive who was promoted into a leadership position only to fail at the job. And they also know a story about someone with solid—but not extraordinary—intellectual abilities and technical skills who was promoted into a similar position and then soared.

Such anecdotes support the widespread belief that identifying individuals with the "right stuff" to be leaders is more art than science. After all, the personal styles of superb leaders vary: Some leaders are subdued and analytical; others shout their manifestos from the mountaintops. And just as important, different situations call for different types of leadership. Most mergers need a sensitive negotiator at the helm, whereas many turnarounds require a more forceful authority.

I have found, however, that the most effective leaders are alike in one crucial way: They all have a high degree of what has come to be known as *emotional intelligence*. It's not that IQ and technical skills are irrelevant. They do matter, but mainly as "threshold capabilities"; that is, they are the entry-level requirements for executive positions. But my research, along with other recent studies, clearly shows that emotional intelligence is the sine qua non of leadership. Without it, a person can have the best training in the world, an incisive, analytical mind, and an endless supply of smart ideas, but he still won't make a great leader.

In the course of the past year, my colleagues and I have focused on how emotional intelligence operates at work. We have examined the relationship between emotional intelligence and effective performance, especially in leaders. And we have observed how emotional intelligence shows itself on the job. How can you tell if someone has high emotional intelligence, for example, and how can you recognize it in yourself? In the following pages, we'll explore these questions, taking each of the components of emotional intelligence—self-awareness, self-regulation, motivation, empathy, and social skill—in turn.

Evaluating Emotional Intelligence

Most large companies today have employed trained psychologists to develop what are known as "competency models" to aid them in identifying, training, and promoting likely stars in the leadership firmament. The psychologists have also developed such models for lower-level positions. And in recent years, I have analyzed competency models from 188 companies, most of which were large and global and included the likes of Lucent Technologies, British Airways, and Credit Suisse.

In carrying out this work, my objective was to determine which personal capabilities drove outstanding performance within these organizations, and to what degree they did so. I grouped capabilities into three categories: purely technical skills like accounting and business planning; cognitive abilities like analytical reasoning; and competencies demonstrating emotional intelligence, such as the ability to work with others and effectiveness in leading change.

To create some of the competency models, psychologists asked senior managers at the companies to identify the capabilities that typified the organization's most outstanding leaders. To create other models, the psychologists used objective criteria, such as a division's profitability, to differentiate the star performers at senior levels within their organizations from the average ones. Those individuals were then extensively interviewed and tested, and their capabilities were compared. This process resulted in the creation of

Idea in Brief

What distinguishes great leaders from merely good ones? It isn't IQ or technical skills, says Daniel Goleman. It's **emotional intelligence (EI)**: a group of five skills that enable the best leaders to maximize their own *and* their followers' performance. When senior managers at one company had a critical mass of EI capabilities, their divisions outperformed yearly earnings goals by 20%.

The EI skills are:

- *Self-awareness*—knowing one's strengths, weaknesses, drives, values, and impact on others

- *Self-regulation*—controlling or redirecting disruptive impulses and moods

- *Motivation*—relishing achievement for its own sake

- *Empathy*—understanding other people's emotional makeup

- *Social skill*—building rapport with others to move them in desired directions

We're each born with certain levels of EI skills. But we can strengthen these abilities through persistence, practice, and feedback from colleagues or coaches.

lists of ingredients for highly effective leaders. The lists ranged in length from seven to 15 items and included such ingredients as initiative and strategic vision.

When I analyzed all this data, I found dramatic results. To be sure, intellect was a driver of outstanding performance. Cognitive skills such as big-picture thinking and long-term vision were particularly important. But when I calculated the ratio of technical skills, IQ, and emotional intelligence as ingredients of excellent performance, emotional intelligence proved to be twice as important as the others for jobs at all levels.

Moreover, my analysis showed that emotional intelligence played an increasingly important role at the highest levels of the company, where differences in technical skills are of negligible importance. In other words, the higher the rank of a person considered to be a star performer, the more emotional intelligence capabilities showed up as the reason for his or her effectiveness. When I compared star performers with average ones in senior leadership positions, nearly 90% of the difference in their profiles was attributable to emotional intelligence factors rather than cognitive abilities.

Idea in Practice

Understanding EI's Components

EI component	Definition	Hallmarks	Example
Self-awareness	Knowing one's emotions, strengths, weaknesses, drives, values, and goals—and their impact on others	• Self-confidence • Realistic self-assessment • Self-deprecating sense of humor • Thirst for constructive criticism	A manager knows tight deadlines bring out the worst in him. So he plans his time to get work done well in advance.
Self-regulation	Controlling or redirecting disruptive emotions and impulses	• Trustworthiness • Integrity • Comfort with ambiguity and change	When a team botches a presentation, its leader resists the urge to scream. Instead, she considers possible reasons for the failure, explains the consequences to her team, and explores solutions with them.
Motivation	Being driven to achieve for the sake of achievement	• A passion for the work itself and for new challenges • Unflagging energy to improve • Optimism in the face of failure	A portfolio manager at an investment company sees his fund tumble for three consecutive quarters. Major clients defect. Instead of blaming external circumstances, she decides to learn from the experience—and engineers a turnaround.

EI component	Definition	Hallmarks	Example
Empathy	Considering others' feelings, especially when making decisions	• Expertise in attracting and retaining talent • Ability to develop others • Sensitivity to cross-cultural differences	An American consultant and her team pitch a project to a potential client in Japan. Her team interprets the client's silence as disapproval, and prepares to leave. The consultant reads the client's body language and senses interest. She continues the meeting, and her team gets the job.
Social skill	Managing relationships to move people in desired directions	• Effectiveness in leading change • Persuasiveness • Extensive networking • Expertise in building and leading teams	A manager wants his company to adopt a better internet strategy. He finds kindred spirits and assembles a de facto team to create a prototype Web site. He persuades allies in other divisions to fund the company's participation in a relevant convention. His company forms an internet division—and puts him in charge of it.

Strengthening Your EI

Use practice and feedback from others to strengthen specific EI skills.

Example: An executive learned from others that she lacked empathy, especially the ability to listen. She wanted to fix the problem, so she asked a coach to tell her when she exhibited poor listening skills. She then role-played incidents to practice giving better responses; for example, not interrupting. She also began observing executives skilled at listening—and imitated their behavior.

The five components of emotional intelligence at work

	Definition	Hallmarks
Self-awareness	The ability to recognize and understand your moods, emotions, and drives, as well as their effect on others	Self-confidence Realistic self-assessment Self-deprecating sense of humor
Self-regulation	The ability to control or redirect disruptive impulses and moods The propensity to suspend judgment—to think before acting	Trustworthiness and integrity Comfort with ambiguity Openness to change
Motivation	A passion to work for reasons that go beyond money or status A propensity to pursue goals with energy and persistence	Strong drive to achieve Optimism, even in the face of failure Organizational commitment
Empathy	The ability to understand the emotional makeup of other people Skill in treating people according to their emotional reactions	Expertise in building and retaining talent Cross-cultural sensitivity Service to clients and customers
Social skill	Proficiency in managing relationships and building networks An ability to find common ground and build rapport	Effectiveness in leading change Persuasiveness Expertise in building and leading teams

Other researchers have confirmed that emotional intelligence not only distinguishes outstanding leaders but can also be linked to strong performance. The findings of the late David McClelland, the renowned researcher in human and organizational behavior, are a good example. In a 1996 study of a global food and beverage company, McClelland found that when senior managers had a critical mass of emotional intelligence capabilities, their divisions outperformed yearly earnings goals by 20%. Meanwhile, division leaders without that critical mass underperformed by almost the same amount. McClelland's findings, interestingly, held as true in the company's U.S. divisions as in its divisions in Asia and Europe.

In short, the numbers are beginning to tell us a persuasive story about the link between a company's success and the emotional intelligence of its leaders. And just as important, research is also demonstrating that people can, if they take the right approach, develop their emotional intelligence. (See the sidebar "Can Emotional Intelligence Be Learned?")

Self-Awareness

Self-awareness is the first component of emotional intelligence—which makes sense when one considers that the Delphic oracle gave the advice to "know thyself" thousands of years ago. Self-awareness means having a deep understanding of one's emotions, strengths, weaknesses, needs, and drives. People with strong self-awareness are neither overly critical nor unrealistically hopeful. Rather, they are honest—with themselves and with others.

People who have a high degree of self-awareness recognize how their feelings affect them, other people, and their job performance. Thus, a self-aware person who knows that tight deadlines bring out the worst in him plans his time carefully and gets his work done well in advance. Another person with high self-awareness will be able to work with a demanding client. She will understand the client's impact on her moods and the deeper reasons for her frustration. "Their trivial demands take us away from the real work that needs to be

Can Emotional Intelligence Be Learned?

FOR AGES, PEOPLE HAVE DEBATED if leaders are born or made. So too goes the debate about emotional intelligence. Are people born with certain levels of empathy, for example, or do they acquire empathy as a result of life's experiences? The answer is both. Scientific inquiry strongly suggests that there is a genetic component to emotional intelligence. Psychological and developmental research indicates that nurture plays a role as well. How much of each perhaps will never be known, but research and practice clearly demonstrate that emotional intelligence can be learned.

One thing is certain: Emotional intelligence increases with age. There is an old-fashioned word for the phenomenon: maturity. Yet even with maturity, some people still need training to enhance their emotional intelligence. Unfortunately, far too many training programs that intend to build leadership skills—including emotional intelligence—are a waste of time and money. The problem is simple: They focus on the wrong part of the brain.

Emotional intelligence is born largely in the neurotransmitters of the brain's limbic system, which governs feelings, impulses, and drives. Research indicates that the limbic system learns best through motivation, extended practice, and feedback. Compare this with the kind of learning that goes on in the neocortex, which governs analytical and technical ability. The neocortex grasps concepts and logic. It is the part of the brain that figures out how to use a computer or make a sales call by reading a book. Not surprisingly—but mistakenly—it is also the part of the brain targeted by most training programs aimed at enhancing emotional intelligence. When such programs take, in effect, a neocortical approach, my research with the Consortium for Research on Emotional Intelligence in Organizations has shown they can even have a *negative* impact on people's job performance.

To enhance emotional intelligence, organizations must refocus their training to include the limbic system. They must help people break old behavioral habits and establish new ones. That not only takes much more time than conventional training programs, it also requires an individualized approach.

Imagine an executive who is thought to be low on empathy by her colleagues. Part of that deficit shows itself as an inability to listen; she interrupts people and doesn't pay close attention to what they're saying. To fix the problem, the executive needs to be motivated to change, and then she needs practice and feedback from others in the company. A colleague or coach could be tapped to let the executive know when she has been observed failing to listen. She would then have to replay the incident and give a better response; that is, demonstrate her ability to absorb what others are saying. And the executive could be directed to observe certain executives who listen well and to mimic their behavior.

With persistence and practice, such a process can lead to lasting results. I know one Wall Street executive who sought to improve his empathy—specifically his ability to read people's reactions and see their perspectives. Before beginning his quest, the executive's subordinates were terrified of working with him. People even went so far as to hide bad news from him. Naturally, he was shocked when finally confronted with these facts. He went home and told his family—but they only confirmed what he had heard at work. When their opinions on any given subject did not mesh with his, they, too, were frightened of him.

Enlisting the help of a coach, the executive went to work to heighten his empathy through practice and feedback. His first step was to take a vacation to a foreign country where he did not speak the language. While there, he monitored his reactions to the unfamiliar and his openness to people who were different from him. When he returned home, humbled by his week abroad, the executive asked his coach to shadow him for parts of the day, several times a week, to critique how he treated people with new or different perspectives. At the same time, he consciously used on-the-job interactions as opportunities to practice "hearing" ideas that differed from his. Finally, the executive had himself videotaped in meetings and asked those who worked for and with him to critique his ability to acknowledge and understand the feelings of others. It took several months, but the executive's emotional intelligence did ultimately rise, and the improvement was reflected in his overall performance on the job.

It's important to emphasize that building one's emotional intelligence cannot—will not—happen without sincere desire and concerted effort. A brief seminar won't help; nor can one buy a how-to manual. It is much harder to learn to empathize—to internalize empathy as a natural response to people—than it is to become adept at regression analysis. But it can be done. "Nothing great was ever achieved without enthusiasm," wrote Ralph Waldo Emerson. If your goal is to become a real leader, these words can serve as a guidepost in your efforts to develop high emotional intelligence.

done," she might explain. And she will go one step further and turn her anger into something constructive.

Self-awareness extends to a person's understanding of his or her values and goals. Someone who is highly self-aware knows where he is headed and why; so, for example, he will be able to be firm in turning down a job offer that is tempting financially but does not fit with his principles or long-term goals. A person who lacks self-awareness is apt to make decisions that bring on inner turmoil by treading on buried values. "The money looked good so I signed on," someone might say two years into a job, "but the work means so little to me that I'm constantly bored." The decisions of self-aware people mesh with their values; consequently, they often find work to be energizing.

How can one recognize self-awareness? First and foremost, it shows itself as candor and an ability to assess oneself realistically. People with high self-awareness are able to speak accurately and openly—although not necessarily effusively or confessionally—about their emotions and the impact they have on their work. For instance, one manager I know of was skeptical about a new personal-shopper service that her company, a major department-store chain, was about to introduce. Without prompting from her team or her boss, she offered them an explanation: "It's hard for me to get behind the rollout of this service," she admitted, "because I really wanted to run the project, but I wasn't selected. Bear with me while I deal with that." The manager did indeed examine her feelings; a week later, she was supporting the project fully.

Such self-knowledge often shows itself in the hiring process. Ask a candidate to describe a time he got carried away by his feelings and did something he later regretted. Self-aware candidates will be frank in admitting to failure—and will often tell their tales with a smile. One of the hallmarks of self-awareness is a self-deprecating sense of humor.

Self-awareness can also be identified during performance reviews. Self-aware people know—and are comfortable talking about—their limitations and strengths, and they often demonstrate a thirst for constructive criticism. By contrast, people with low self-awareness interpret the message that they need to improve as a threat or a sign of failure.

Self-aware people can also be recognized by their self-confidence. They have a firm grasp of their capabilities and are less likely to set themselves up to fail by, for example, overstretching on assignments. They know, too, when to ask for help. And the risks they take on the job are calculated. They won't ask for a challenge that they know they can't handle alone. They'll play to their strengths.

Consider the actions of a midlevel employee who was invited to sit in on a strategy meeting with her company's top executives. Although she was the most junior person in the room, she did not sit there quietly, listening in awestruck or fearful silence. She knew she had a head for clear logic and the skill to present ideas persuasively, and she offered cogent suggestions about the company's strategy. At the same time, her self-awareness stopped her from wandering into territory where she knew she was weak.

Despite the value of having self-aware people in the workplace, my research indicates that senior executives don't often give self-awareness the credit it deserves when they look for potential leaders. Many executives mistake candor about feelings for "wimpiness" and fail to give due respect to employees who openly acknowledge their shortcomings. Such people are too readily dismissed as "not tough enough" to lead others.

In fact, the opposite is true. In the first place, people generally admire and respect candor. Furthermore, leaders are constantly required to make judgment calls that require a candid assessment of capabilities—their own and those of others. Do we have the management expertise to acquire a competitor? Can we launch a new product within six months? People who assess themselves honestly—that is, self-aware people—are well suited to do the same for the organizations they run.

Self-Regulation

Biological impulses drive our emotions. We cannot do away with them—but we can do much to manage them. Self-regulation, which is like an ongoing inner conversation, is the component of emotional intelligence that frees us from being prisoners of our feelings. People engaged in such a conversation feel bad moods and emotional impulses just as everyone else does, but they find ways to control them and even to channel them in useful ways.

Imagine an executive who has just watched a team of his employees present a botched analysis to the company's board of directors. In the gloom that follows, the executive might find himself tempted to pound on the table in anger or kick over a chair. He could leap up and scream at the group. Or he might maintain a grim silence, glaring at everyone before stalking off.

But if he had a gift for self-regulation, he would choose a different approach. He would pick his words carefully, acknowledging the team's poor performance without rushing to any hasty judgment. He would then step back to consider the reasons for the failure. Are they personal—a lack of effort? Are there any mitigating factors? What was his role in the debacle? After considering these questions, he would call the team together, lay out the incident's consequences, and offer his feelings about it. He would then present his analysis of the problem and a well-considered solution.

Why does self-regulation matter so much for leaders? First of all, people who are in control of their feelings and impulses—that is, people who are reasonable—are able to create an environment of trust and fairness. In such an environment, politics and infighting are sharply reduced and productivity is high. Talented people flock to the organization and aren't tempted to leave. And self-regulation has a trickle-down effect. No one wants to be known as a hothead when the boss is known for her calm approach. Fewer bad moods at the top mean fewer throughout the organization.

Second, self-regulation is important for competitive reasons. Everyone knows that business today is rife with ambiguity and change. Companies merge and break apart regularly. Technology transforms work at a dizzying pace. People who have mastered their emotions are able to roll with the changes. When a new program is announced, they don't panic; instead, they are able to suspend judgment, seek out information, and listen to the executives as they explain the new program. As the initiative moves forward, these people are able to move with it.

Sometimes they even lead the way. Consider the case of a manager at a large manufacturing company. Like her colleagues, she had used a certain software program for five years. The program drove how she collected and reported data and how she thought about the company's strategy. One day, senior executives announced that a new program was to be installed that would radically change how information was gathered and assessed within the organization. While many people in the company complained bitterly about how disruptive the change would be, the manager mulled over the reasons for the new program and was convinced of its potential to improve performance. She eagerly attended training sessions—some of her colleagues refused to do so—and was eventually promoted to run several divisions, in part because she used the new technology so effectively.

I want to push the importance of self-regulation to leadership even further and make the case that it enhances integrity, which is not only a personal virtue but also an organizational strength. Many of the bad things that happen in companies are a function of impulsive behavior. People rarely plan to exaggerate profits, pad expense accounts, dip into the till, or abuse power for selfish ends. Instead, an opportunity presents itself, and people with low impulse control just say yes.

By contrast, consider the behavior of the senior executive at a large food company. The executive was scrupulously honest in his negotiations with local distributors. He would routinely lay out his cost structure in detail, thereby giving the distributors a realistic understanding of the company's pricing. This approach meant the executive couldn't always drive a hard bargain. Now, on occasion, he felt the urge to increase profits by withholding information about the company's costs. But he challenged that impulse—he saw that it made more sense in the long run to counteract it. His emotional self-regulation paid off in strong, lasting relationships with distributors that benefited the company more than any short-term financial gains would have.

The signs of emotional self-regulation, therefore, are easy to see: a propensity for reflection and thoughtfulness; comfort with ambiguity and change; and integrity—an ability to say no to impulsive urges.

Like self-awareness, self-regulation often does not get its due. People who can master their emotions are sometimes seen as cold fish—their considered responses are taken as a lack of passion. People with fiery temperaments are frequently thought of as "classic" leaders—their outbursts are considered hallmarks of charisma and power. But when such people make it to the top, their impulsiveness often works against them. In my research, extreme displays of negative emotion have never emerged as a driver of good leadership.

Motivation

If there is one trait that virtually all effective leaders have, it is motivation. They are driven to achieve beyond expectations—their own and everyone else's. The key word here is *achieve*. Plenty of people are motivated by external factors, such as a big salary or the status that comes from having an impressive title or being part of a prestigious company. By contrast, those with leadership potential are motivated by a deeply embedded desire to achieve for the sake of achievement.

If you are looking for leaders, how can you identify people who are motivated by the drive to achieve rather than by external rewards? The first sign is a passion for the work itself—such people seek out creative challenges, love to learn, and take great pride in a job well done. They also display an unflagging energy to do things better. People with such energy often seem restless with the status quo. They are persistent with their questions about why things are done one way rather than another; they are eager to explore new approaches to their work.

A cosmetics company manager, for example, was frustrated that he had to wait two weeks to get sales results from people in the field. He finally tracked down an automated phone system that would beep each of his salespeople at 5 pm every day. An automated message then prompted them to punch in their numbers—how many calls and sales they had made that day. The system shortened the feedback time on sales results from weeks to hours.

That story illustrates two other common traits of people who are driven to achieve. They are forever raising the performance bar, and they like to keep score. Take the performance bar first. During performance reviews, people with high levels of motivation might ask to be "stretched" by their superiors. Of course, an employee who combines self-awareness with internal motivation will recognize her limits—but she won't settle for objectives that seem too easy to fulfill.

And it follows naturally that people who are driven to do better also want a way of tracking progress—their own, their team's, and their company's. Whereas people with low achievement motivation are often fuzzy about results, those with high achievement motivation often keep score by tracking such hard measures as profitability or market share. I know of a money manager who starts and ends his day on the Internet, gauging the performance of his stock fund against four industry-set benchmarks.

Interestingly, people with high motivation remain optimistic even when the score is against them. In such cases, self-regulation combines with achievement motivation to overcome the frustration and depression that come after a setback or failure. Take the case of another portfolio manager at a large investment company. After several successful years, her fund tumbled for three consecutive quarters, leading three large institutional clients to shift their business elsewhere.

Some executives would have blamed the nosedive on circumstances outside their control; others might have seen the setback as evidence of personal failure. This portfolio manager, however, saw an opportunity to prove she could lead a turnaround. Two years later, when she was promoted to a very senior level in the company, she described the experience as "the best thing that ever happened to me; I learned so much from it."

Executives trying to recognize high levels of achievement motivation in their people can look for one last piece of evidence: commitment to the organization. When people love their jobs for the work itself, they often feel committed to the organizations that

93

make that work possible. Committed employees are likely to stay with an organization even when they are pursued by headhunters waving money.

It's not difficult to understand how and why a motivation to achieve translates into strong leadership. If you set the performance bar high for yourself, you will do the same for the organization when you are in a position to do so. Likewise, a drive to surpass goals and an interest in keeping score can be contagious. Leaders with these traits can often build a team of managers around them with the same traits. And of course, optimism and organizational commitment are fundamental to leadership—just try to imagine running a company without them.

Empathy

Of all the dimensions of emotional intelligence, empathy is the most easily recognized. We have all felt the empathy of a sensitive teacher or friend; we have all been struck by its absence in an unfeeling coach or boss. But when it comes to business, we rarely hear people praised, let alone rewarded, for their empathy. The very word seems unbusinesslike, out of place amid the tough realities of the marketplace.

But empathy doesn't mean a kind of "I'm OK, you're OK" mushiness. For a leader, that is, it doesn't mean adopting other people's emotions as one's own and trying to please everybody. That would be a nightmare—it would make action impossible. Rather, empathy means thoughtfully considering employees' feelings—along with other factors—in the process of making intelligent decisions.

For an example of empathy in action, consider what happened when two giant brokerage companies merged, creating redundant jobs in all their divisions. One division manager called his people together and gave a gloomy speech that emphasized the number of people who would soon be fired. The manager of another division gave his people a different kind of speech. He was up-front about his own worry and confusion, and he promised to keep people informed and to treat everyone fairly.

The difference between these two managers was empathy. The first manager was too worried about his own fate to consider the feelings of his anxiety-stricken colleagues. The second knew intuitively what his people were feeling, and he acknowledged their fears with his words. Is it any surprise that the first manager saw his division sink as many demoralized people, especially the most talented, departed? By contrast, the second manager continued to be a strong leader, his best people stayed, and his division remained as productive as ever.

Empathy is particularly important today as a component of leadership for at least three reasons: the increasing use of teams; the rapid pace of globalization; and the growing need to retain talent.

Consider the challenge of leading a team. As anyone who has ever been a part of one can attest, teams are cauldrons of bubbling emotions. They are often charged with reaching a consensus—which is hard enough with two people and much more difficult as the numbers increase. Even in groups with as few as four or five members, alliances form and clashing agendas get set. A team's leader must be able to sense and understand the viewpoints of everyone around the table.

That's exactly what a marketing manager at a large information technology company was able to do when she was appointed to lead a troubled team. The group was in turmoil, overloaded by work and missing deadlines. Tensions were high among the members. Tinkering with procedures was not enough to bring the group together and make it an effective part of the company.

So the manager took several steps. In a series of one-on-one sessions, she took the time to listen to everyone in the group—what was frustrating them, how they rated their colleagues, whether they felt they had been ignored. And then she directed the team in a way that brought it together: She encouraged people to speak more openly about their frustrations, and she helped people raise constructive complaints during meetings. In short, her empathy allowed her to understand her team's emotional makeup. The result was not just heightened collaboration among members but also added business, as the team was called on for help by a wider range of internal clients.

Globalization is another reason for the rising importance of empathy for business leaders. Cross-cultural dialogue can easily lead to miscues and misunderstandings. Empathy is an antidote. People who have it are attuned to subtleties in body language; they can hear the message beneath the words being spoken. Beyond that, they have a deep understanding of both the existence and the importance of cultural and ethnic differences.

Consider the case of an American consultant whose team had just pitched a project to a potential Japanese client. In its dealings with Americans, the team was accustomed to being bombarded with questions after such a proposal, but this time it was greeted with a long silence. Other members of the team, taking the silence as disapproval, were ready to pack and leave. The lead consultant gestured them to stop. Although he was not particularly familiar with Japanese culture, he read the client's face and posture and sensed not rejection but interest—even deep consideration. He was right: When the client finally spoke, it was to give the consulting firm the job.

Finally, empathy plays a key role in the retention of talent, particularly in today's information economy. Leaders have always needed empathy to develop and keep good people, but today the stakes are higher. When good people leave, they take the company's knowledge with them.

That's where coaching and mentoring come in. It has repeatedly been shown that coaching and mentoring pay off not just in better performance but also in increased job satisfaction and decreased turnover. But what makes coaching and mentoring work best is the nature of the relationship. Outstanding coaches and mentors get inside the heads of the people they are helping. They sense how to give effective feedback. They know when to push for better performance and when to hold back. In the way they motivate their protégés, they demonstrate empathy in action.

In what is probably sounding like a refrain, let me repeat that empathy doesn't get much respect in business. People wonder how leaders can make hard decisions if they are "feeling" for all the people who will be affected. But leaders with empathy do more than sympathize with people around them: They use their knowledge to improve their companies in subtle but important ways.

Social Skill

The first three components of emotional intelligence are self-management skills. The last two, empathy and social skill, concern a person's ability to manage relationships with others. As a component of emotional intelligence, social skill is not as simple as it sounds. It's not just a matter of friendliness, although people with high levels of social skill are rarely mean-spirited. Social skill, rather, is friendliness with a purpose: moving people in the direction you desire, whether that's agreement on a new marketing strategy or enthusiasm about a new product.

Socially skilled people tend to have a wide circle of acquaintances, and they have a knack for finding common ground with people of all kinds—a knack for building rapport. That doesn't mean they socialize continually; it means they work according to the assumption that nothing important gets done alone. Such people have a network in place when the time for action comes.

Social skill is the culmination of the other dimensions of emotional intelligence. People tend to be very effective at managing relationships when they can understand and control their own emotions and can empathize with the feelings of others. Even motivation contributes to social skill. Remember that people who are driven to achieve tend to be optimistic, even in the face of setbacks or failure. When people are upbeat, their "glow" is cast upon conversations and other social encounters. They are popular, and for good reason.

Because it is the outcome of the other dimensions of emotional intelligence, social skill is recognizable on the job in many ways that will by now sound familiar. Socially skilled people, for instance, are adept at managing teams—that's their empathy at work. Likewise, they are expert persuaders—a manifestation of self-awareness, self-regulation, and empathy combined. Given those skills, good persuaders know when to make an emotional plea, for instance, and when an appeal to reason will work better. And motivation, when publicly visible, makes such people excellent collaborators; their passion for the work spreads to others, and they are driven to find solutions.

But sometimes social skill shows itself in ways the other emotional intelligence components do not. For instance, socially skilled people may at times appear not to be working while at work. They seem to be idly schmoozing—chatting in the hallways with colleagues or joking around with people who are not even connected to their "real" jobs. Socially skilled people, however, don't think it makes sense to arbitrarily limit the scope of their relationships. They build bonds widely because they know that in these fluid times, they may need help someday from people they are just getting to know today.

For example, consider the case of an executive in the strategy department of a global computer manufacturer. By 1993, he was convinced that the company's future lay with the Internet. Over the course of the next year, he found kindred spirits and used his social skill to stitch together a virtual community that cut across levels, divisions, and nations. He then used this de facto team to put up a corporate Web site, among the first by a major company. And, on his own initiative, with no budget or formal status, he signed up the company to participate in an annual Internet industry convention. Calling on his allies and persuading various divisions to donate funds, he recruited more than 50 people from a dozen different units to represent the company at the convention.

Management took notice: Within a year of the conference, the executive's team formed the basis for the company's first Internet division, and he was formally put in charge of it. To get there, the executive had ignored conventional boundaries, forging and maintaining connections with people in every corner of the organization.

Is social skill considered a key leadership capability in most companies? The answer is yes, especially when compared with the other components of emotional intelligence. People seem to know intuitively that leaders need to manage relationships effectively;

no leader is an island. After all, the leader's task is to get work done through other people, and social skill makes that possible. A leader who cannot express her empathy may as well not have it at all. And a leader's motivation will be useless if he cannot communicate his passion to the organization. Social skill allows leaders to put their emotional intelligence to work.

It would be foolish to assert that good-old-fashioned IQ and technical ability are not important ingredients in strong leadership. But the recipe would not be complete without emotional intelligence. It was once thought that the components of emotional intelligence were "nice to have" in business leaders. But now we know that, for the sake of performance, these are ingredients that leaders "need to have."

It is fortunate, then, that emotional intelligence can be learned. The process is not easy. It takes time and, most of all, commitment. But the benefits that come from having a well-developed emotional intelligence, both for the individual and for the organization, make it worth the effort.

Originally published in June 1996. Reprint R0401H

The Authenticity Paradox

by Herminia Ibarra

AUTHENTICITY HAS BECOME THE GOLD standard for leadership. But a simplistic understanding of what it means can hinder your growth and limit your impact.

Consider Cynthia, a general manager in a health care organization. Her promotion into that role increased her direct reports 10-fold and expanded the range of businesses she oversaw—and she felt a little shaky about making such a big leap. A strong believer in transparent, collaborative leadership, she bared her soul to her new employees: "I want to do this job," she said, "but it's scary, and I need your help." Her candor backfired; she lost credibility with people who wanted and needed a confident leader to take charge.

Or take George, a Malaysian executive in an auto parts company where people valued a clear chain of command and made decisions by consensus. When a Dutch multinational with a matrix structure acquired the company, George found himself working with peers who saw decision making as a freewheeling contest for the best-debated ideas. That style didn't come easily to him, and it contradicted everything he had learned about humility growing up in his country. In a 360-degree debrief, his boss told him that he needed to sell his ideas and accomplishments more aggressively. George felt he had to choose between being a failure and being a fake.

Because going against our natural inclinations can make us feel like impostors, we tend to latch on to authenticity as an excuse for sticking with what's comfortable. But few jobs allow us to do that for long. That's doubly true when we advance in our careers or when demands or expectations change, as Cynthia, George, and countless other executives have discovered.

In my research on leadership transitions, I have observed that career advances require all of us to move way beyond our comfort zones. At the same time, however, they trigger a strong countervailing impulse to protect our identities: When we are unsure of ourselves or our ability to perform well or measure up in a new setting, we often retreat to familiar behaviors and styles.

But my research also demonstrates that the moments that most challenge our sense of self are the ones that can teach us the most about leading effectively. By viewing ourselves as works in progress and evolving our professional identities through trial and error, we can develop a personal style that feels right to us and suits our organizations' changing needs.

That takes courage, because learning, by definition, starts with unnatural and often superficial behaviors that can make us feel calculating instead of genuine and spontaneous. But the only way to avoid being pigeonholed and ultimately become better leaders is to do the things that a rigidly authentic sense of self would keep us from doing.

Why Leaders Struggle with Authenticity

The word "authentic" traditionally referred to any work of art that is an original, not a copy. When used to describe leadership, of course, it has other meanings—and they can be problematic. For example, the notion of adhering to one "true self" flies in the face of much research on how people evolve with experience, discovering facets of themselves they would never have unearthed through introspection alone. And being utterly transparent—disclosing every single thought and feeling—is both unrealistic and risky.

Idea in Brief

The Problem

When we view authenticity as an unwavering sense of self, we struggle to take on new challenges and bigger roles. The reality is that people learn—and change—who they are through experience.

The Solution

By trying out different leadership styles and behaviors, we grow more than we would through introspection alone. Experimenting with our identities allows us to find the right approach for ourselves and our organizations.

The Sticking Point

This adaptive approach to authenticity can make us feel like impostors, because it involves doing things that may not come naturally. But it's outside our comfort zones that we learn the most about leading effectively.

Leaders today struggle with authenticity for several reasons. First, we make more-frequent and more-radical changes in the kinds of work we do. As we strive to *improve* our game, a clear and firm sense of self is a compass that helps us navigate choices and progress toward our goals. But when we're looking to *change* our game, a too rigid self-concept becomes an anchor that keeps us from sailing forth, as it did at first with Cynthia.

Second, in global business, many of us work with people who don't share our cultural norms and have different expectations for how we should behave. It can often seem as if we have to choose between what is expected—and therefore effective—and what feels authentic. George is a case in point.

Third, identities are always on display in today's world of ubiquitous connectivity and social media. How we present ourselves—not just as executives but as people, with quirks and broader interests—has become an important aspect of leadership. Having to carefully curate a persona that's out there for all to see can clash with our private sense of self.

In dozens of interviews with talented executives facing new expectations, I have found that they most often grapple with authenticity in the following situations.

Taking charge in an unfamiliar role

As everyone knows, the first 90 days are critical in a new leadership role. First impressions form quickly, and they matter. Depending on their personalities, leaders respond very differently to the increased visibility and performance pressure.

Psychologist Mark Snyder, of the University of Minnesota, identified two psychological profiles that inform how leaders develop their personal styles. "High self-monitors"—or chameleons, as I call them—are naturally able and willing to adapt to the demands of a situation without feeling fake. Chameleons care about managing their public image and often mask their vulnerability with bluster. They may not always get it right the first time, but they keep trying on different styles like new clothes until they find a good fit for themselves and their circumstances. Because of that flexibility, they often advance rapidly. But chameleons can run into problems when people perceive them as disingenuous or lacking a moral center—even though they're expressing their "true" chameleon nature.

By contrast, "true-to-selfers" (Snyder's "low self-monitors") tend to express what they really think and feel, even when it runs counter to situational demands. The danger with true-to-selfers like Cynthia and George is that they may stick too long with comfortable behavior that prevents them from meeting new requirements, instead of evolving their style as they gain insight and experience.

Cynthia (whom I interviewed after her story appeared in a *Wall Street Journal* article by Carol Hymowitz) hemmed herself in like this. She thought she was setting herself up for success by staying true to her highly personal, full-disclosure style of management. She asked her new team for support, openly acknowledging that she felt a bit at sea. As she scrambled to learn unfamiliar aspects of the business, she worked tirelessly to contribute to every decision and solve every problem. After a few months, she was on the verge of burnout. To make matters worse, sharing her vulnerability with her team members so early on had damaged her standing. Reflecting on her transition some years later, Cynthia told me: "Being authentic doesn't mean that you can be held up to the light and people can see right through you." But at the time, that was how she saw it—and instead of building trust, she made people question her ability to do the job.

Delegating and communicating appropriately are only part of the problem in a case like this. A deeper-seated issue is finding the right mix of distance and closeness in an unfamiliar situation. Stanford psychologist Deborah Gruenfeld describes this as managing the tension between authority and approachability. To be authoritative, you privilege your knowledge, experience, and expertise over the team's, maintaining a measure of distance. To be approachable, you emphasize your relationships with people, their input, and their perspective, and you lead with empathy and warmth. Getting the balance right presents an acute authenticity crisis for true-to-selfers, who typically have a strong preference for behaving one way or the other. Cynthia made herself too approachable and vulnerable, and it undermined and drained her. In her bigger role, she needed more distance from her employees to gain their confidence and get the job done.

Selling your ideas (and yourself)

Leadership growth usually involves a shift from having good ideas to pitching them to diverse stakeholders. Inexperienced leaders, especially true-to-selfers, often find the process of getting buy-in distasteful because it feels artificial and political; they believe that their work should stand on its own merits.

Here's an example: Anne, a senior manager at a transportation company, had doubled revenue and fundamentally redesigned core processes in her unit. Despite her obvious accomplishments, however, her boss didn't consider her an inspirational leader. Anne also knew she was not communicating effectively in her role as a board member of the parent company. The chairman, a broad-brush thinker, often became impatient with her detail orientation. His feedback to her was "step up, do the vision thing." But to Anne that seemed like valuing form over substance. "For me, it is manipulation," she told me in an interview. "I can do the storytelling too, but I refuse to play on people's emotions. If the string-pulling is too obvious, I can't make myself do it." Like many aspiring leaders, she resisted crafting emotional messages to influence and inspire others because that felt less authentic to her than relying on facts, figures, and spreadsheets. As a result, she worked at cross-purposes with the board chairman, pushing hard on the facts instead of pulling him in as a valued ally.

Many managers know deep down that their good ideas and strong potential will go unnoticed if they don't do a better job of selling themselves. Still, they can't bring themselves to do it. "I try to build a network based on professionalism and what I can deliver for the business, not who I know," one manager told me. "Maybe that's not smart from a career point of view. But I can't go against my beliefs. . . . So I have been more limited in 'networking up.'"

Until we see career advancement as a way of extending our reach and increasing our impact in the organization—a collective win, not just a selfish pursuit—we have trouble feeling authentic when touting our strengths to influential people. True-to-selfers find it particularly hard to sell themselves to senior management when they most need to do so: when they are still unproven. Research shows, however, that this hesitancy disappears as people gain experience and become more certain of the value they bring.

Processing negative feedback

Many successful executives encounter serious negative feedback for the first time in their careers when they take on larger roles or responsibilities. Even when the criticisms aren't exactly new, they loom larger because the stakes are higher. But leaders often convince themselves that dysfunctional aspects of their "natural" style are the inevitable price of being effective.

Let's look at Jacob, a food company production manager whose direct reports gave him low marks in a 360 review on emotional intelligence, team building, and empowering others. One team member wrote that it was hard for Jacob to accept criticism. Another remarked that after an angry outburst, he'd suddenly make a joke as if nothing had happened, not realizing the destabilizing effect of his mood

Why Companies Are Pushing Authenticity Training

MANAGERS CAN CHOOSE from countless books, articles, and executive workshops for advice on how to be more authentic at work. Two trends help explain the exploding popularity of the concept and the training industry it has fed.

First, trust in business leaders fell to an all-time low in 2012, according to the Edelman Trust Barometer. Even in 2013, when trust began to climb back up, only 18% of people reported that they trusted business leaders to tell the truth, and fewer than half trusted businesses to do the right thing.

Second, employee engagement is at a nadir. A 2013 Gallup poll found that only 13% of employees worldwide are engaged at work. Only one in eight workers—out of roughly 180 million employees studied—is psychologically committed to his or her job. In study after study, frustration, burnout, disillusionment, and misalignment with personal values are cited among the biggest reasons for career change.

At a time when public confidence and employee morale are so low, it's no surprise that companies are encouraging leaders to discover their "true" selves.

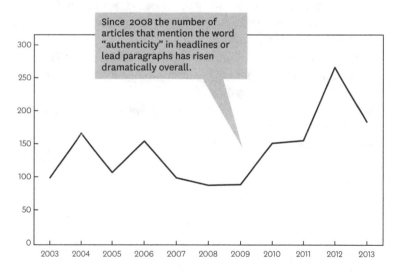

Since 2008 the number of articles that mention the word "authenticity" in headlines or lead paragraphs has risen dramatically overall.

Source: *New York Times, Financial Times, Washington Post, Economist, Forbes, Wall Street Journal,* and *HBR*

changes on those around him. For someone who genuinely believed that he'd built trust among his people, all this was tough to swallow.

Once the initial shock had subsided, Jacob acknowledged that this was not the first time he'd received such criticism (some colleagues and subordinates had made similar comments a few years earlier). "I thought I'd changed my approach," he reflected, "but I haven't really changed so much since the last time." However, he quickly rationalized his behavior to his boss: "Sometimes you have to be tough in order to deliver results, and people don't like it," he said. "You have to accept that as part of the job description." Of course, he was missing the point.

Because negative feedback given to leaders often centers on style rather than skills or expertise, it can feel like a threat to their identity—as if they're being asked to give up their "secret sauce." That's how Jacob saw it. Yes, he could be explosive—but from his point of view, his "toughness" allowed him to deliver results year after year. In reality, though, he had succeeded up to this point *despite* his behavior. When his role expanded and he took on greater responsibility, his intense scrutiny of subordinates became an even bigger obstacle because it took up time he should have been devoting to more-strategic pursuits.

A great public example of this phenomenon is Margaret Thatcher. Those who worked with her knew she could be merciless if someone failed to prepare as thoroughly as she did. She was capable of humiliating a staff member in public, she was a notoriously bad listener, and she believed that compromise was cowardice. As she became known to the world as the "Iron Lady," Thatcher grew more and more convinced of the rightness of her ideas and the necessity of her coercive methods. She could beat anyone into submission with the power of her rhetoric and conviction, and she only got better at it. Eventually, though, it was her undoing—she was ousted by her own cabinet.

A Playful Frame of Mind

Such a rigid self-concept can result from too much introspection. When we look only within for answers, we inadvertently reinforce old ways of seeing the world and outdated views of ourselves.

Without the benefit of what I call outsight—the valuable external perspective we get from experimenting with new leadership behaviors—habitual patterns of thought and action fence us in. To begin thinking like leaders, we must first act: plunge ourselves into new projects and activities, interact with very different kinds of people, and experiment with new ways of getting things done. Especially in times of transition and uncertainty, thinking and introspection should follow experience—not vice versa. Action changes who we are and what we believe is worth doing.

Fortunately, there are ways of increasing outsight and evolving toward an "adaptively authentic" way of leading, but they require a playful frame of mind. Think of leadership development as trying on possible selves rather than working on yourself—which, let's face it, sounds like drudgery. When we adopt a playful attitude, we're more open to possibilities. It's OK to be inconsistent from one day to the next. That's not being a fake; it's how we experiment to figure out what's right for the new challenges and circumstances we face.

My research suggests three important ways to get started.

Learn from diverse role models

Most learning necessarily involves some form of imitation—and the understanding that nothing is "original." An important part of growing as a leader is viewing authenticity not as an intrinsic state but as the ability to take elements you have learned from others' styles and behaviors and make them your own.

But don't copy just one person's leadership style; tap many diverse role models. There is a big difference between imitating someone wholesale and borrowing selectively from various people to create your own collage, which you then modify and improve. As the playwright Wilson Mizner said, copying one author is plagiarism, but copying many is research.

I observed the importance of this approach in a study of investment bankers and consultants who were advancing from analytical and project work to roles advising clients and selling new business. Though most of them felt incompetent and insecure in their new positions, the chameleons among them consciously borrowed styles and tactics from successful senior leaders—learning through emulation how to use humor to break tension in meetings, for instance, and how to shape opinion without being overbearing. Essentially, the chameleons faked it until they found what worked for them. Noticing their efforts, their managers provided coaching and mentoring and shared tacit knowledge.

As a result, the chameleons arrived much faster at an authentic but more skillful style than the true-to-selfers in the study, who continued to focus solely on demonstrating technical mastery. Often the true-to-selfers concluded that their managers were "all talk and little content" and therefore not suitable role models. In the absence of a "perfect" model they had a harder time with imitation—it felt bogus. Unfortunately, their managers perceived their inability to adapt as a lack of effort or investment and thus didn't give them as much mentoring and coaching as they gave the chameleons.

Work on getting better

Setting goals for learning (not just for performance) helps us experiment with our identities without feeling like impostors, because we don't expect to get everything right from the start. We stop trying to protect our comfortable old selves from the threats that change can bring, and start exploring what kinds of leaders we might become.

Of course, we all want to perform well in a new situation—get the right strategy in place, execute like crazy, deliver results the organization cares about. But focusing exclusively on those things makes us afraid to take risks in the service of learning. In a series of ingenious experiments, Stanford psychologist Carol Dweck has shown that concern about how we will appear to others inhibits learning on new or unfamiliar tasks. Performance goals motivate us to show others that we possess valued attributes, such as intelligence and social skill, and to prove to ourselves that we have them. By contrast, learning goals motivate us to develop valued attributes.

The Cultural Factor

WHATEVER THE SITUATION—TAKING charge in unfamiliar territory, selling your ideas and yourself, or processing negative feedback—finding authentic ways of being effective is even more difficult in a multicultural environment.

As my INSEAD colleague Erin Meyer finds in her research, styles of persuading others and the kinds of arguments that people find persuasive are far from universal; they are deeply rooted in a culture's philosophical, religious, and educational assumptions. That said, prescriptions for how leaders are supposed to look and sound are rarely as diverse as the leaders themselves. And despite corporate initiatives to build understanding of cultural differences and promote diversity, the fact is that leaders are still expected to express ideas assertively, to claim credit for them, and to use charisma to motivate and inspire people.

Authenticity is supposed to be an antidote to a single model of leadership. (After all, the message is to be yourself, not what someone else expects you to be.) But as the notion has gained currency, it has, ironically, come to mean something much more limiting and culturally specific. A closer look at how leaders are taught to discover and demonstrate authenticity—by telling a personal story about a hardship they have overcome, for example—reveals a model that is, in fact, very American, based on ideals such as self-disclosure, humility, and individualistic triumph over adversity.

This amounts to a catch-22 for managers from cultures with different norms for authority, communication, and collective endeavor because they must behave inauthentically in order to conform to the strictures of "authentic" leadership.

When we're in performance mode, leadership is about presenting ourselves in the most favorable light. In learning mode, we can reconcile our yearning for authenticity in how we work and lead with an equally powerful desire to grow. One leader I met was highly effective in small-group settings but struggled to convey openness to new ideas in larger meetings, where he often stuck to long-winded presentations for fear of getting derailed by others' comments. He set himself a "no PowerPoint" rule to develop a more relaxed, improvisational style. He surprised himself by how much he learned, not only about his own evolving preferences but also about the issues at hand.

Don't stick to "your story"

Most of us have personal narratives about defining moments that taught us important lessons. Consciously or not, we allow our stories, and the images of ourselves that they paint, to guide us in new situations. But the stories can become outdated as we grow, so sometimes it's necessary to alter them dramatically or even to throw them out and start from scratch.

That was true for Maria, a leader who saw herself as a "mother hen with her chicks all around." Her coach, former Ogilvy & Mather CEO Charlotte Beers, explains in *I'd Rather Be in Charge* that this self-image emerged from a time when Maria had to sacrifice her own goals and dreams to take care of her extended family. It eventually began to hold her back in her career: Though it had worked for her as a friendly and loyal team player and a peacekeeper, it wasn't helping her get the big leadership assignment she wanted. Together Maria and her coach looked for another defining moment to use as a touchstone—one that was more in keeping with Maria's desired future self, not who she had been in the past. They chose the time when Maria, as a young woman, had left her family to travel the world for 18 months. Acting from that bolder sense of self, she asked for—and got—a promotion that had previously been elusive.

Dan McAdams, a Northwestern psychology professor who has spent his career studying life stories, describes identity as "the internalized and evolving story that results from a person's selective appropriation of past, present and future." This isn't just academic jargon. McAdams is saying that you have to believe your story—but also embrace how it changes over time, according to what you need it to do. Try out new stories about yourself, and keep editing them, much as you would your résumé.

Again, revising one's story is both an introspective and a social process. The narratives we choose should not only sum up our experiences and aspirations but also reflect the demands we face and resonate with the audience we're trying to win over.

———————

Countless books and advisers tell you to start your leadership journey with a clear sense of who you are. But that can be a recipe for staying stuck in the past. Your leadership identity can and should change each time you move on to bigger and better things.

The only way we grow as leaders is by stretching the limits of who we are—doing new things that make us uncomfortable but that teach us through direct experience who we want to become. Such growth doesn't require a radical personality makeover. Small changes—in the way we carry ourselves, the way we communicate, the way we interact—often make a world of difference in how effectively we lead.

Originally published in January–February 2015. Reprint R1501C

Managing Your Boss

by John J. Gabarro and John P. Kotter

TO MANY PEOPLE, THE PHRASE "managing your boss" may sound unusual or suspicious. Because of the traditional top-down emphasis in most organizations, it is not obvious why you need to manage relationships upward—unless, of course, you would do so for personal or political reasons. But we are not referring to political maneuvering or to apple polishing. We are using the term to mean the process of consciously working with your superior to obtain the best possible results for you, your boss, and the company.

Recent studies suggest that effective managers take time and effort to manage not only relationships with their subordinates but also those with their bosses. These studies also show that this essential aspect of management is sometimes ignored by otherwise talented and aggressive managers. Indeed, some managers who actively and effectively supervise subordinates, products, markets, and technologies assume an almost passively reactive stance vis-à-vis their bosses. Such a stance almost always hurts them and their companies.

If you doubt the importance of managing your relationship with your boss or how difficult it is to do so effectively, consider for a moment the following sad but telling story:

Frank Gibbons was an acknowledged manufacturing genius in his industry and, by any profitability standard, a very effective executive. In 1973, his strengths propelled him into the position of vice president of manufacturing for the second largest and most profitable company in its industry. Gibbons was not, however, a good manager of people. He knew this, as did others in his company and his industry. Recognizing this weakness, the president made sure that those who reported to Gibbons were good at working with people and could compensate for his limitations. The arrangement worked well.

In 1975, Philip Bonnevie was promoted into a position reporting to Gibbons. In keeping with the previous pattern, the president selected Bonnevie because he had an excellent track record and a reputation for being good with people. In making that selection, however, the president neglected to notice that, in his rapid rise through the organization, Bonnevie had always had good-to-excellent bosses. He had never been forced to manage a relationship with a difficult boss. In retrospect, Bonnevie admits he had never thought that managing his boss was a part of his job.

Fourteen months after he started working for Gibbons, Bonnevie was fired. During that same quarter, the company reported a net loss for the first time in seven years. Many of those who were close to these events say that they don't really understand what happened. This much is known, however: While the company was bringing out a major new product—a process that required sales, engineering, and manufacturing groups to coordinate decisions very carefully—a whole series of misunderstandings and bad feelings developed between Gibbons and Bonnevie.

For example, Bonnevie claims Gibbons was aware of and had accepted Bonnevie's decision to use a new type of machinery to make the new product; Gibbons swears he did not. Furthermore, Gibbons claims he made it clear to Bonnevie that the introduction of the product was too important to the company in the short run to take any major risks.

As a result of such misunderstandings, planning went awry: A new manufacturing plant was built that could not produce the new product designed by engineering, in the volume desired by sales, at a cost agreed on by the executive committee. Gibbons blamed Bonnevie for the mistake. Bonnevie blamed Gibbons.

Idea in Brief

Managing our *bosses*? Isn't that merely manipulation? Corporate cozying up? Out-and-out apple polishing? In fact, we manage our bosses for very good reasons: to get resources to do the best job, not only for ourselves, but for our bosses and our companies as well. We actively pursue a healthy and productive working relationship based on mutual respect and understanding—understanding our own and our bosses' strengths, weaknesses, goals, work styles, and needs. Here's what can happen when we don't:

> *Example:* A new president with a formal work style replaced someone who'd been looser, more intuitive. The new president preferred written reports and structured meetings. One of his managers found this too controlling. He seldom sent background information, and was often blindsided by unanticipated questions. His boss found their meetings inefficient and frustrating. The manager had to resign.

In contrast, here's how another manager's sensitivity to this same boss's style really paid off:

> *Example:* This manager identified the kinds and frequency of information the president wanted. He sent ahead background reports and discussion agendas. The result? Highly productive meetings and even more innovative problem solving than with his previous boss.

Managers often don't realize how much their bosses depend on them. They need cooperation, reliability, and honesty from their direct reports. Many managers also don't realize how much *they* depend on their bosses—for links to the rest of the organization, for setting priorities, and for obtaining critical resources.

Recognizing this mutual dependence, effective managers seek out information about the boss's concerns and are sensitive to his work style. They also understand how their own attitudes toward authority can sabotage the relationship. Some see the boss as the enemy and fight him at every turn; others are overly compliant, viewing the boss as an all-wise parent.

Of course, one could argue that the problem here was caused by Gibbons's inability to manage his subordinates. But one can make just as strong a case that the problem was related to Bonnevie's inability to manage his boss. Remember, Gibbons was not having difficulty with any other subordinates. Moreover, given the personal

Idea in Practice

You can benefit from this mutual dependence and develop a very productive relationship with your boss by focusing on:

- **Compatible work styles.** Bosses process information differently. "Listeners" prefer to be briefed in person so they can ask questions. "Readers" want to process written information first, and then meet to discuss.

Decision-making styles also vary. Some bosses are highly involved. Touch base with them frequently. Others prefer to delegate. Inform them about important decisions you've already made.

- **Mutual expectations.** Don't passively assume you know what the boss expects. Find out. With some bosses, write detailed outlines of your work for their approval. With others, carefully planned discussions are key.

Also, communicate *your* expectations to find out if they are realistic. Persuade the boss to accept the most important ones.

- **Information flow.** Managers typically underestimate what their bosses need to know—and what they *do* know. Keep the boss informed through processes that fit his style. Be forthright about both good and bad news.

- **Dependability and honesty.** Trustworthy subordinates only make promises they can keep and don't shade the truth or play down difficult issues.

- **Good use of time and resources.** Don't waste your boss's time with trivial issues. Selectively draw on his time and resources to meet the most important goals—yours, his, and the company's.

price paid by Bonnevie (being fired and having his reputation within the industry severely tarnished), there was little consolation in saying the problem was that Gibbons was poor at managing subordinates. Everyone already knew that.

We believe that the situation could have turned out differently had Bonnevie been more adept at understanding Gibbons and at managing his relationship with him. In this case, an inability to manage upward was unusually costly. The company lost $2 million to $5 million, and Bonnevie's career was, at least temporarily, disrupted. Many less costly cases similar to this probably occur regularly in all major corporations, and the cumulative effect can be very destructive.

Misreading the Boss–Subordinate Relationship

People often dismiss stories like the one we just related as being merely cases of personality conflict. Because two people can on occasion be psychologically or temperamentally incapable of working together, this can be an apt description. But more often, we have found, a personality conflict is only a part of the problem— sometimes a very small part.

Bonnevie did not just have a different personality from Gibbons, he also made or had unrealistic assumptions and expectations about the very nature of boss-subordinate relationships. Specifically, he did not recognize that his relationship to Gibbons involved *mutual dependence* between two *fallible* human beings. Failing to recognize this, a manager typically either avoids trying to manage his or her relationship with a boss or manages it ineffectively.

Some people behave as if their bosses were not very dependent on them. They fail to see how much the boss needs their help and cooperation to do his or her job effectively. These people refuse to acknowledge that the boss can be severely hurt by their actions and needs cooperation, dependability, and honesty from them.

Some people see themselves as not very dependent on their bosses. They gloss over how much help and information they need from the boss in order to perform their own jobs well. This superficial view is particularly damaging when a manager's job and decisions affect other parts of the organization, as was the case in Bonnevie's situation. A manager's immediate boss can play a critical role in linking the manager to the rest of the organization, making sure the manager's priorities are consistent with organizational needs, and in securing the resources the manager needs to perform well. Yet some managers need to see themselves as practically self-sufficient, as not needing the critical information and resources a boss can supply.

Many managers, like Bonnevie, assume that the boss will magically know what information or help their subordinates need and provide it to them. Certainly, some bosses do an excellent job of caring for their subordinates in this way, but for a manager to expect that from all bosses is dangerously unrealistic. A more reasonable expectation for managers to have is that modest help will be forthcoming. After all, bosses are only human. Most really effective managers accept this fact and assume primary responsibility for their own careers and development. They make a point of seeking the information and help they need to do a job instead of waiting for their bosses to provide it.

In light of the foregoing, it seems to us that managing a situation of mutual dependence among fallible human beings requires the following:

1. You have a good understanding of the other person and yourself, especially regarding strengths, weaknesses, work styles, and needs.

2. You use this information to develop and manage a healthy working relationship—one that is compatible with both people's work styles and assets, is characterized by mutual expectations, and meets the most critical needs of the other person.

This combination is essentially what we have found highly effective managers doing.

Understanding the Boss

Managing your boss requires that you gain an understanding of the boss and his or her context, as well as your own situation. All managers do this to some degree, but many are not thorough enough.

At a minimum, you need to appreciate your boss's goals and pressures, his or her strengths and weaknesses. What are your boss's organizational and personal objectives, and what are his or her pressures, especially those from his or her own boss and others at the same level? What are your boss's long suits and blind spots? What is the preferred style of working? Does your boss like to get information through memos, formal meetings, or phone calls? Does he or she thrive on conflict or try to minimize it? Without this information, a manager is flying blind when dealing with the boss, and unnecessary conflicts, misunderstandings, and problems are inevitable.

In one situation we studied, a top-notch marketing manager with a superior performance record was hired into a company as a vice president "to straighten out the marketing and sales problems." The company, which was having financial difficulties, had recently been acquired by a larger corporation. The president was eager to turn it around and gave the new marketing vice president free rein—at least initially. Based on his previous experience, the new vice president correctly diagnosed that greater market share was needed for the company and that strong product management was required to bring that about. Following that logic, he made a number of pricing decisions aimed at increasing high-volume business.

When margins declined and the financial situation did not improve, however, the president increased pressure on the new vice president. Believing that the situation would eventually correct itself as the company gained back market share, the vice president resisted the pressure.

When by the second quarter, margins and profits had still failed to improve, the president took direct control over all pricing decisions and put all items on a set level of margin, regardless of volume. The new vice president began to find himself shut out by the president, and their relationship deteriorated. In fact, the vice president found the president's behavior bizarre. Unfortunately, the president's new pricing scheme also failed to increase margins, and by the fourth quarter, both the president and the vice president were fired.

What the new vice president had not known until it was too late was that improving marketing and sales had been only *one* of the president's goals. His most immediate goal had been to make the company more profitable—quickly.

Nor had the new vice president known that his boss was invested in this short-term priority for personal as well as business reasons. The president had been a strong advocate of the acquisition within the parent company, and his personal credibility was at stake.

The vice president made three basic errors. He took information supplied to him at face value, he made assumptions in areas where he had no information, and—what was most damaging—he never actively tried to clarify what his boss's objectives were. As a result, he ended up taking actions that were actually at odds with the president's priorities and objectives.

Managers who work effectively with their bosses do not behave this way. They seek out information about the boss's goals and problems and pressures. They are alert for opportunities to question the boss and others around him or her to test their assumptions. They pay attention to clues in the boss's behavior. Although it is imperative that they do this especially when they begin working with a new boss, effective managers also do this on an ongoing basis because they recognize that priorities and concerns change.

Being sensitive to a boss's work style can be crucial, especially when the boss is new. For example, a new president who was organized and formal in his approach replaced a man who was informal and intuitive. The new president worked best when he had written reports. He also preferred formal meetings with set agendas.

One of his division managers realized this need and worked with the new president to identify the kinds and frequency of information and reports that the president wanted. This manager also made a point of sending background information and brief agendas ahead of time for their discussions. He found that with this type of preparation their meetings were very useful. Another interesting result was, he found that with adequate preparation his new boss was even more effective at brainstorming problems than his more informal and intuitive predecessor had been.

In contrast, another division manager never fully understood how the new boss's work style differed from that of his predecessor. To the degree that he did sense it, he experienced it as too much control. As a result, he seldom sent the new president the background information he needed, and the president never felt fully prepared for meetings with the manager. In fact, the president spent much of the time when they met trying to get information that he felt he should have had earlier. The boss experienced these meetings as frustrating and inefficient, and the subordinate often found himself thrown off guard by the questions that the president asked. Ultimately, this division manager resigned.

The difference between the two division managers just described was not so much one of ability or even adaptability. Rather, one of the men was more sensitive to his boss's work style and to the implications of his boss's needs than the other was.

Understanding Yourself

The boss is only one-half of the relationship. You are the other half, as well as the part over which you have more direct control. Developing an effective working relationship requires, then, that you know your own needs, strengths and weaknesses, and personal style.

You are not going to change either your basic personality structure or that of your boss. But you can become aware of what it is about you that impedes or facilitates working with your boss and, with that awareness, take actions that make the relationship more effective.

For example, in one case we observed, a manager and his superior ran into problems whenever they disagreed. The boss's typical response was to harden his position and overstate it. The manager's reaction was then to raise the ante and intensify the forcefulness of his argument. In doing this, he channeled his anger into sharpening his attacks on the logical fallacies he saw in his boss's assumptions. His boss in turn would become even more adamant about holding his original position. Predictably, this escalating cycle resulted in the subordinate avoiding whenever possible any topic of potential conflict with his boss.

In discussing this problem with his peers, the manager discovered that his reaction to the boss was typical of how he generally reacted to counterarguments—but with a difference. His response would overwhelm his peers but not his boss. Because his attempts to discuss this problem with his boss were unsuccessful, he concluded that the only way to change the situation was to deal with his own instinctive reactions. Whenever the two reached an impasse, he would check his own impatience and suggest that they break up and think about it before getting together again. Usually when they renewed their discussion, they had digested their differences and were more able to work them through.

Gaining this level of self-awareness and acting on it are difficult but not impossible. For example, by reflecting over his past experiences, a young manager learned that he was not very good at dealing with difficult and emotional issues where people were involved. Because he disliked those issues and realized that his instinctive responses to them were seldom very good, he developed a habit of touching base with his boss whenever such a problem arose. Their discussions always surfaced ideas and approaches the manager had not considered. In many cases, they also identified specific actions the boss could take to help.

Although a superior-subordinate relationship is one of mutual dependence, it is also one in which the subordinate is typically more dependent on the boss than the other way around. This dependence inevitably results in the subordinate feeling a certain degree of frustration, sometimes anger, when his actions or options are constrained by his boss's decisions. This is a normal part of life and occurs in the best of relationships. The way in which a manager handles these frustrations largely depends on his or her predisposition toward dependence on authority figures.

Some people's instinctive reaction under these circumstances is to resent the boss's authority and to rebel against the boss's decisions. Sometimes a person will escalate a conflict beyond what is appropriate. Seeing the boss almost as an institutional enemy, this type of manager will often, without being conscious of it, fight with the boss just for the sake of fighting. The subordinate's reactions to being constrained are usually strong and sometimes impulsive. He or she sees the boss as someone who, by virtue of the role, is a hindrance to progress, an obstacle to be circumvented or at best tolerated.

Psychologists call this pattern of reactions counterdependent behavior. Although a counterdependent person is difficult for most superiors to manage and usually has a history of strained relationships with superiors, this sort of manager is apt to have even more trouble with a boss who tends to be directive or authoritarian. When the manager acts on his or her negative feelings, often in subtle and nonverbal ways, the boss sometimes does become the enemy. Sensing the subordinate's latent hostility, the boss will lose trust in the subordinate or his or her judgment and then behave even less openly.

Paradoxically, a manager with this type of predisposition is often a good manager of his or her own people. He or she will many times go out of the way to get support for them and will not hesitate to go to bat for them.

At the other extreme are managers who swallow their anger and behave in a very compliant fashion when the boss makes what they know to be a poor decision. These managers will agree with the boss even when a disagreement might be welcome or when the boss would easily alter a decision if given more information. Because they bear no relationship to the specific situation at hand, their responses are as much an overreaction as those of counterdependent managers. Instead of seeing the boss as an enemy, these people deny their anger—the other extreme—and tend to see the boss as if he or she were an all-wise parent who should know best, should take responsibility for their careers, train them in all they need to know, and protect them from overly ambitious peers.

Both counterdependence and overdependence lead managers to hold unrealistic views of what a boss is. Both views ignore that bosses, like everyone else, are imperfect and fallible. They don't have unlimited time, encyclopedic knowledge, or extrasensory perception; nor are they evil enemies. They have their own pressures and concerns that are sometimes at odds with the wishes of the subordinate—and often for good reason.

Altering predispositions toward authority, especially at the extremes, is almost impossible without intensive psychotherapy (psychoanalytic theory and research suggest that such predispositions are deeply rooted in a person's personality and upbringing). However, an awareness of these extremes and the range between them can be very useful in understanding where your own predispositions fall and what the implications are for how you tend to behave in relation to your boss.

If you believe, on the one hand, that you have some tendencies toward counterdependence, you can understand and even predict what your reactions and overreactions are likely to be. If, on the other hand, you believe you have some tendencies toward overdependence, you might question the extent to which your overcompliance or inability to confront real differences may be making both you and your boss less effective.

Developing and Managing the Relationship

With a clear understanding of both your boss and yourself, you can *usually* establish a way of working together that fits both of you, that is characterized by unambiguous mutual expectations, and that helps you both be more productive and effective. The "Checklist for Managing Your Boss" summarizes some things such a relationship consists of. Following are a few more.

Checklist for Managing Your Boss

Make sure you understand your boss and his or her context, including:

☐ Goals and objectives

☐ Pressures

☐ Strengths, weaknesses, blind spots

☐ Preferred work style

Assess yourself and your needs, including:

☐ Strengths and weaknesses

☐ Personal style

☐ Predisposition toward dependence on authority figures

Develop and maintain a relationship that:

☐ Fits both your needs and styles

☐ Is characterized by mutual expectations

☐ Keeps your boss informed

☐ Is based on dependability and honesty

☐ Selectively uses your boss's time and resources

Compatible work styles

Above all else, a good working relationship with a boss accommodates differences in work style. For example, in one situation we studied, a manager (who had a relatively good relationship with his superior) realized that during meetings his boss would often become inattentive and sometimes brusque. The subordinate's own style tended to be discursive and exploratory. He would often digress from the topic at hand to deal with background factors, alternative approaches, and so forth. His boss preferred to discuss problems with a minimum of background detail and became impatient and distracted whenever his subordinate digressed from the immediate issue.

Recognizing this difference in style, the manager became terser and more direct during meetings with his boss. To help himself do this, before meetings, he would develop brief agendas that he used as a guide. Whenever he felt that a digression was needed, he explained why. This small shift in his own style made these meetings more effective and far less frustrating for both of them.

Subordinates can adjust their styles in response to their bosses' preferred method for receiving information. Peter Drucker divides bosses into "listeners" and "readers." Some bosses like to get information in report form so they can read and study it. Others work better with information and reports presented in person so they can ask questions. As Drucker points out, the implications are obvious. If your boss is a listener, you brief him or her in person, *then* follow it up with a memo. If your boss is a reader, you cover important items or proposals in a memo or report, *then* discuss them.

Other adjustments can be made according to a boss's decision-making style. Some bosses prefer to be involved in decisions and problems as they arise. These are high-involvement managers who like to keep their hands on the pulse of the operation. Usually their needs (and your own) are best satisfied if you touch base with them on an ad hoc basis. A boss who has a need to be involved will become involved one way or another, so there are advantages to including him or her at your initiative. Other bosses prefer to delegate—they don't want to be involved. They expect you to come to them with major problems and inform them about any important changes.

Creating a compatible relationship also involves drawing on each other's strengths and making up for each other's weaknesses. Because he knew that the boss—the vice president of engineering—was not very good at monitoring his employees' problems, one manager we studied made a point of doing it himself. The stakes were high: The engineers and technicians were all union members, the company worked on a customer-contract basis, and the company had recently experienced a serious strike.

The manager worked closely with his boss, along with people in the scheduling department and the personnel office, to make sure that potential problems were avoided. He also developed an informal arrangement through which his boss would review with him any proposed changes in personnel or assignment policies before taking action. The boss valued his advice and credited his subordinate for improving both the performance of the division and the labor-management climate.

Mutual expectations

The subordinate who passively assumes that he or she knows what the boss expects is in for trouble. Of course, some superiors will spell out their expectations very explicitly and in great detail. But most do not. And although many corporations have systems that provide a basis for communicating expectations (such as formal planning processes, career planning reviews, and performance appraisal reviews), these systems never work perfectly. Also, between these formal reviews, expectations invariably change.

Ultimately, the burden falls on the subordinate to find out what the boss's expectations are. They can be both broad (such as what kinds of problems the boss wishes to be informed about and when) as well as very specific (such things as when a particular project should be completed and what kinds of information the boss needs in the interim).

Getting a boss who tends to be vague or not explicit to express expectations can be difficult. But effective managers find ways to get that information. Some will draft a detailed memo covering key aspects of their work and then send it to their boss for approval. They then follow this up with a face-to-face discussion in which they go over each item in the memo. A discussion like this will often surface virtually all of the boss's expectations.

Other effective managers will deal with an inexplicit boss by initiating an ongoing series of informal discussions about "good management" and "our objectives." Still others find useful information more indirectly through those who used to work for the boss and through the formal planning systems in which the boss makes commitments to his or her own superior. Which approach you choose, of course, should depend on your understanding of your boss's style.

Developing a workable set of mutual expectations also requires that you communicate your own expectations to the boss, find out if they are realistic, and influence the boss to accept the ones that are important to you. Being able to influence the boss to value your expectations can be particularly important if the boss is an overachiever. Such a boss will often set unrealistically high standards that need to be brought into line with reality.

A flow of information
How much information a boss needs about what a subordinate is doing will vary significantly depending on the boss's style, the situation he or she is in, and the confidence the boss has in the subordinate. But it is not uncommon for a boss to need more information than the subordinate would naturally supply or for the subordinate to think the boss knows more than he or she really does. Effective managers recognize that they probably underestimate what their bosses need to know and make sure they find ways to keep them informed through processes that fit their styles.

Managing the flow of information upward is particularly difficult if the boss does not like to hear about problems. Although many people would deny it, bosses often give off signals that they want to hear only good news. They show great displeasure—usually nonverbally—when someone tells them about a problem. Ignoring individual achievement, they may even evaluate more favorably subordinates who do not bring problems to them.

Nevertheless, for the good of the organization, the boss, and the subordinate, a superior needs to hear about failures as well as successes. Some subordinates deal with a good-news-only boss by finding indirect ways to get the necessary information to him or her, such as a management information system. Others see to it that potential problems, whether in the form of good surprises or bad news, are communicated immediately.

Dependability and honesty

Few things are more disabling to a boss than a subordinate on whom he cannot depend, whose work he cannot trust. Almost no one is intentionally undependable, but many managers are inadvertently so because of oversight or uncertainty about the boss's priorities. A commitment to an optimistic delivery date may please a superior in the short term but become a source of displeasure if not honored. It's difficult for a boss to rely on a subordinate who repeatedly slips deadlines. As one president (describing a subordinate) put it: "I'd rather he be more consistent even if he delivered fewer peak successes—at least I could rely on him."

Nor are many managers intentionally dishonest with their bosses. But it is easy to shade the truth and play down issues. Current concerns often become future surprise problems. It's almost impossible for bosses to work effectively if they cannot rely on a fairly accurate reading from their subordinates. Because it undermines credibility, dishonesty is perhaps the most troubling trait a subordinate can have. Without a basic level of trust, a boss feels compelled to check all of a subordinate's decisions, which makes it difficult to delegate.

Good use of time and resources

Your boss is probably as limited in his or her store of time, energy, and influence as you are. Every request you make of your boss uses up some of these resources, so it's wise to draw on these resources selectively. This may sound obvious, but many managers use up their boss's time (and some of their own credibility) over relatively trivial issues.

One vice president went to great lengths to get his boss to fire a meddlesome secretary in another department. His boss had to use considerable influence to do it. Understandably, the head of the other department was not pleased. Later, when the vice president wanted to tackle more important problems, he ran into trouble. By using up blue chips on a relatively trivial issue, he had made it difficult for him and his boss to meet more important goals.

No doubt, some subordinates will resent that on top of all their other duties, they also need to take time and energy to manage their relationships with their bosses. Such managers fail to realize the importance of this activity and how it can simplify their jobs by eliminating potentially severe problems. Effective managers recognize that this part of their work is legitimate. Seeing themselves as ultimately responsible for what they achieve in an organization, they know they need to establish and manage relationships with everyone on whom they depend—and that includes the boss.

Originally published in January 1980. Reprint R0501J

How Leaders Create and Use Networks

by Herminia Ibarra and Mark Lee Hunter

WHEN HENRIK BALMER BECAME THE production manager and a board member of a newly bought-out cosmetics firm, improving his network was the last thing on his mind. The main problem he faced was time: Where would he find the hours to guide his team through a major upgrade of the production process and then think about strategic issues like expanding the business? The only way he could carve out time and still get home to his family at a decent hour was to lock himself—literally—in his office. Meanwhile, there were day-to-day issues to resolve, like a recurring conflict with his sales director over custom orders that compromised production efficiency. Networking, which Henrik defined as the unpleasant task of trading favors with strangers, was a luxury he could not afford. But when a new acquisition was presented at a board meeting without his input, he abruptly realized he was out of the loop—not just inside the company, but outside, too—at a moment when his future in the company was at stake.

Henrik's case is not unusual. Over the past two years, we have been following a cohort of 30 managers making their way through what we call the leadership transition, an inflection point in their careers that challenges them to rethink both themselves and their roles. In the process, we've found that networking—creating a fabric of personal contacts who will provide support, feedback, insight, resources, and information—is simultaneously one of the most self-evident and one of the most dreaded developmental challenges that aspiring leaders must address.

Their discomfort is understandable. Typically, managers rise through the ranks by dint of a strong command of the technical elements of their jobs and a nose-to-the-grindstone focus on accomplishing their teams' objectives. When challenged to move beyond their functional specialties and address strategic issues facing the overall business, many managers do not immediately grasp that this will involve relational—not analytical—tasks. Nor do they easily understand that exchanges and interactions with a diverse array of current and potential stakeholders are not distractions from their "real work" but are actually at the heart of their new leadership roles.

Like Henrik (whose identity we've disguised, along with all the other managers we describe here), a majority of the managers we work with say that they find networking insincere or manipulative—at best, an elegant way of using people. Not surprisingly, for every manager who instinctively constructs and maintains a useful network, we see several who struggle to overcome this innate resistance. Yet the alternative to networking is to fail—either in reaching for a leadership position or in succeeding at it.

Watching our emerging leaders approach this daunting task, we discovered that three distinct but interdependent forms of networking—*operational, personal,* and *strategic*—played a vital role in their transitions. The first helped them manage current internal responsibilities, the second boosted their personal development, and the third opened their eyes to new business directions and the stakeholders they would need to enlist. While our managers differed in how well they pursued operational and personal networking, we discovered that almost all of them underutilized strategic networking. In this article, we describe key features of each networking form (summarized in the table "The Three Forms of Networking") and, using our managers' experiences, explain how a three-pronged networking strategy can become part and parcel of a new leader's development plan.

Idea in Brief

What separates successful leaders from the rest of the pack? Networking: creating a tissue of personal contacts to provide the support, feedback, and resources needed to get things done.

Yet many leaders avoid networking. Some think they don't have time for it. Others disdain it as manipulative.

To succeed as a leader, Ibarra and Hunter recommend building three types of networks:

- **Operational**—people you need to accomplish your assigned, routine tasks.

- **Personal**—kindred spirits outside your organization who can help you with personal advancement.

- **Strategic**—people outside your control who will enable you to reach key organizational objectives.

You need all three types of networks. But to *really* succeed, you must master strategic networking—by interacting regularly with people who can open your eyes to new business opportunities and help you capitalize on them. Build your strategic network, and burnish your own—and your company's—performance.

Operational Networking

All managers need to build good working relationships with the people who can help them do their jobs. The number and breadth of people involved can be impressive—such operational networks include not only direct reports and superiors but also peers within an operational unit, other internal players with the power to block or support a project, and key outsiders such as suppliers, distributors, and customers. The purpose of this type of networking is to ensure coordination and cooperation among people who have to know and trust one another in order to accomplish their immediate tasks. That isn't always easy, but it is relatively straightforward, because the task provides focus and a clear criterion for membership in the network: Either you're necessary to the job and helping to get it done, or you're not.

Although operational networking was the form that came most naturally to the managers we studied, nearly every one had

Idea in Practice

The most effective leaders understand the differences among the three types of networks and how to build them.

	Operational network	Personal network	Strategic network
Network's purpose	Getting work done efficiently.	Develop professional skills through coaching and mentoring; exchange important referrals and needed outside information.	Figure out future priorities and challenges; get stakeholder support for them.
How to find network members	Identify individuals who can block or support a project.	Participate in professional associations, alumni groups, clubs, and personal-interest communities.	Identify lateral and vertical relationships with other functional and business-unit managers—people outside your immediate control—who can help you determine how your role and contribution fit into the overall picture.

important blind spots regarding people and groups they depended on to make things happen. In one case, Alistair, an accounting manager who worked in an entrepreneurial firm with several hundred employees, was suddenly promoted by the company's founder to financial director and given a seat on the board. He was both the youngest and the least-experienced board member, and his instinctive response to these new responsibilities was to reestablish his functional credentials. Acting on a hint from the founder that the company might go public, Alistair undertook a reorganization of the accounting department that would enable the books to withstand close scrutiny. Alistair succeeded brilliantly in upgrading his team's capabilities, but he missed the fact that only a minority of the seven-person board shared the founder's ambition. A year

Leveraging Your Networks

Networking takes work. To lessen the pain and increase the gain:

- **Mind your mind-set.** Accept that networking is one of the most important requirements of a leadership role. To overcome any qualms about it, identify a person you respect who networks effectively and ethically. Observe how he or she uses networks to accomplish goals.

- **Reallocate your time.** Master the art of delegation, to liberate time you can then spend on cultivating networks.

- **Establish connections.** Create reasons for interacting with people outside your function or organization; for instance, by taking advantage of social interests to set the stage for addressing strategic concerns.

  Example: An investment banker invited key clients to the theatre (a passion of hers) several times a year. Through these events, she developed her own business *and* learned things about her clients' companies that generated business and ideas for other divisions in her firm.

- **Give and take continually.** Don't wait until you really need something badly to ask for a favor from a network member. Instead, take every opportunity to give to—and receive from—people in your networks, whether you need help or not.

into Alistair's tenure, discussion about whether to take the company public polarized the board, and he discovered that all that time cleaning up the books might have been better spent sounding out his codirectors.

One of the problems with an exclusive reliance on operational networks is that they are usually geared toward meeting objectives as assigned, not toward asking the strategic question, "What *should* we be doing?" By the same token, managers do not exercise as much personal choice in assembling operational relationships as they do in weaving personal and strategic networks, because to a large extent the right relationships are prescribed by the job and organizational structure. Thus, most operational networking occurs within an organization, and ties are determined in large part by routine, short-term demands. Relationships formed with outsiders, such as board members, customers, and regulators, are directly task-related and tend to be bounded and constrained by demands determined at a higher level. Of course, an individual manager can choose to deepen and develop the ties to different extents, and all managers exercise discretion over who gets priority attention. It's the quality of relationships—the rapport and mutual trust—that gives an operational network its power. Nonetheless, the substantial constraints on network membership mean these connections are unlikely to deliver value to managers beyond assistance with the task at hand.

The typical manager in our group was more concerned with sustaining cooperation within the existing network than with building relationships to face nonroutine or unforeseen challenges. But as a manager moves into a leadership role, his or her network must reorient itself externally and toward the future.

Personal Networking

We observed that once aspiring leaders like Alistair awaken to the dangers of an excessively internal focus, they begin to seek kindred spirits outside their organizations. Simultaneously, they become aware of the limitations of their social skills, such as a lack of knowledge about professional domains beyond their own, which makes it difficult for them to find common ground with people outside their usual circles. Through professional associations, alumni groups, clubs, and personal interest communities, managers gain new perspectives that allow them to advance in their careers. This is what we mean by personal networking.

Many of the managers we study question why they should spend precious time on an activity so indirectly related to the work at hand. Why widen one's circle of casual acquaintances when there isn't time even for urgent tasks? The answer is that these contacts provide important referrals, information, and, often, developmental support such as coaching and mentoring. A newly appointed factory director, for example, faced with a turnaround-or-close-down situation that was paralyzing his staff, joined a business organization—and through it met a lawyer who became his counsel in the turnaround. Buoyed by his success, he networked within his company's headquarters in search of someone who had dealt with a similar crisis. Eventually, he found two mentors.

A personal network can also be a safe space for personal development and as such can provide a foundation for strategic networking. The experience of Timothy, a principal in a midsize software company, is a good example. Like his father, Timothy stuttered. When he had the opportunity to prepare for meetings, his stutter was not an issue, but spontaneous encounters inside and outside the company were dreadfully painful. To solve this problem, he began accepting at least two invitations per week to the social gatherings he had assiduously ignored before. Before each event, he asked who else had been invited and did background research on the other guests so that he could initiate conversations. The hardest part, he said, was "getting through the door." Once inside, his interest in the conversations helped him forget himself and master his stutter. As his stutter diminished, he also applied himself to networking across his company, whereas previously he had taken refuge in his technical expertise. Like Timothy, several of our emerging leaders successfully used personal networking as a relatively safe way to expose problems and seek insight into solutions—safe, that is, compared with strategic networking, in which the stakes are far higher.

Personal networks are largely external, made up of discretionary links to people with whom we have something in common. As a result, what makes a personal network powerful is its referral potential. According to the famous six degrees of separation principle, our personal contacts are valuable to the extent that they help us reach, in as few connections as possible, the far-off person who has the information we need.

In watching managers struggle to widen their professional relationships in ways that feel both natural and legitimate to them, we repeatedly saw them shift their time and energy from operational to personal networking. For people who have rarely looked outside their organizations, this is an important first step, one that fosters a

The Three Forms of Networking

Managers who think they are adept at networking are often operating only at an operational or personal level. Effective leaders learn to employ networks for strategic purposes.

	Operational	Personal	Strategic
Purpose	Getting work done efficiently; maintaining the capacities and functions required of the group.	Enhancing personal and professional development; providing referrals to useful information and contacts.	Figuring out future priorities and challenges; getting stakeholder support for them.
Location and temporal orientation	Contacts are mostly internal and oriented toward current demands.	Contacts are mostly external and oriented toward current interests and future potential interests.	Contacts are internal and external and oriented toward the future.
Players and recruitment	Key contacts are relatively non-discretionary; they are prescribed mostly by the task and organizational structure, so it is very clear who is relevant.	Key contacts are mostly discretionary; it is not always clear who is relevant.	Key contacts follow from the strategic context and the organizational environment, but specific membership is discretionary; it is not always clear who is relevant.
Network attributes and key behaviors	Depth: building strong working relationships.	Breadth: reaching out to contacts who can make referrals.	Leverage: creating inside-outside links.

deeper understanding of themselves and the environments in which they move. Ultimately, however, personal networking alone won't propel managers through the leadership transition. Aspiring leaders may find people who awaken new interests but fail to become comfortable with the power players at the level above them. Or they may achieve new influence within a professional community but fail to harness those ties in the service of organizational goals. That's why managers who know they need to develop their networking skills, and make a real effort to do so, nonetheless may end up feeling like they have wasted their time and energy. As we'll see, personal networking will not help a manager through the leadership transition unless he or she learns how to bring those connections to bear on organizational strategy.

Strategic Networking

When managers begin the delicate transition from functional manager to business leader, they must start to concern themselves with broad strategic issues. Lateral and vertical relationships with other functional and business unit managers—all people outside their immediate control—become a lifeline for figuring out how their own contributions fit into the big picture. Thus strategic networking plugs the aspiring leader into a set of relationships and information sources that collectively embody the power to achieve personal and organizational goals.

Operating beside players with diverse affiliations, backgrounds, objectives, and incentives requires a manager to formulate business rather than functional objectives, and to work through the coalitions and networks needed to sell ideas and compete for resources. Consider Sophie, a manager who, after rising steadily through the ranks in logistics and distribution, was stupefied to learn that the CEO was considering a radical reorganization of her function that would strip her of some responsibilities. Rewarded to date for incremental annual improvements, she had failed to notice shifting priorities in the wider market and the resulting internal shuffle for resources and power at the higher levels of her company. Although she had

From Functional Manager to Business Leader: How Companies Can Help

EXECUTIVES WHO OVERSEE MANAGEMENT development know how to spot critical inflection points: the moments when highly successful people must change their perspective on what is important and, accordingly, how they spend their time. Many organizations still promote people on the basis of their performance in roles whose requirements differ dramatically from those of leadership roles. And many new leaders feel that they are going it alone, without coaching or guidance. By being sensitive to the fact that most strong technical or functional managers lack the capabilities required to build strategic networks that advance their personal and professional goals, human resources and learning professionals can take steps to help in this important area.

For example, Genesis Park, an innovative in-house leadership development program at PricewaterhouseCoopers, focuses explicitly on building networks. The five-month program, during which participants are released from their client responsibilities, includes business case development, strategic projects, team building, change management projects, and in-depth discussions with business leaders from inside and outside the company. The young leaders who participate end up with a strong internal-external nexus of ties to support them as their careers evolve.

---

built a loyal, high-performing team, she had few relationships outside her group to help her anticipate the new imperatives, let alone give her ideas about how to respond. After she argued that distribution issues were her purview, and failed to be persuasive, she hired consultants to help her prepare a counterproposal. But Sophie's boss simply concluded that she lacked a broad, longer-term business perspective. Frustrated, Sophie contemplated leaving the company. Only after some patient coaching from a senior manager did she understand that she had to get out of her unit and start talking to opinion leaders inside and outside the company to form a sellable plan for the future.

What differentiates a leader from a manager, research tells us, is the ability to figure out where to go and to enlist the people and groups necessary to get there. Recruiting stakeholders, lining up allies and sympathizers, diagnosing the political landscape, and brokering conversations among unconnected parties are all part of

Companies that recognize the importance of leadership networking can also do a lot to help people overcome their innate discomfort by creating natural ways for them to extend their networks. When Nissan CEO Carlos Ghosn sought to break down crippling internal barriers at the company, he created cross-functional teams of middle managers from diverse units and charged them with proposing solutions to problems ranging from supply costs to product design. Nissan subsequently institutionalized the teams, not just as a way to solve problems but also to encourage lateral networks. Rather than avoid the extra work, aspiring leaders ask for these assignments.

Most professional development is based on the notion that successful people acquire new role-appropriate skills as they move up the hierarchy. But making the transition from manager to leader requires subtraction as well as addition: To make room for new competencies, managers must rely less on their older, well-honed skills. To do so, they must change their perspective on how to add value and what to contribute. Eventually, they must also transform how they think and who they are. Companies that help their top talent reinvent themselves will better prepare them for a successful leadership transition.

a leader's job. As they step up to the leadership transition, some managers accept their growing dependence on others and seek to transform it into mutual influence. Others dismiss such work as "political" and, as a result, undermine their ability to advance their goals.

Several of the participants in our sample chose the latter approach, justifying their choice as a matter of personal values and integrity. In one case, Jody, who managed a department in a large company under what she described as "dysfunctional" leadership, refused even to try to activate her extensive network within the firm when internal adversaries took over key functions of her unit. When we asked her why she didn't seek help from anyone in the organization to stop this coup, she replied that she refused to play "stupid political games. . . . You can only do what you think is the ethical and right thing from your perspective." Stupid or not, those games cost her the respect and support of her direct reports and coworkers, who hesitated to follow someone they perceived as unwilling to defend herself. Eventually she had no choice but to leave.

The key to a good strategic network is leverage: the ability to marshal information, support, and resources from one sector of a network to achieve results in another. Strategic networkers use indirect influence, convincing one person in the network to get someone else, who is not in the network, to take a needed action. Moreover, strategic networkers don't just influence their relational environment; they shape it in their own image by moving and hiring subordinates, changing suppliers and sources of financing, lobbying to place allies in peer positions, and even restructuring their boards to create networks favorable to their business goals. Jody abjured such tactics, but her adversaries did not.

Strategic networking can be difficult for emerging leaders because it absorbs a significant amount of the time and energy that managers usually devote to meeting their many operational demands. This is one reason why many managers drop their strategic networking precisely when they need it most: when their units are in trouble and only outside support can rescue them. The trick is not to hide in the operational network but to develop it into a more strategic one.

One manager we studied, for example, used lateral and functional contacts throughout his firm to resolve tensions with his boss that resulted from substantial differences in style and strategic approaches between the two. Tied down in operational chores at a distant location, the manager had lost contact with headquarters. He resolved the situation by simultaneously obliging his direct reports to take on more of the local management effort and sending messages through his network that would help bring him back into the loop with the boss.

Operational, personal, and strategic networks are not mutually exclusive. One manager we studied used his personal passion, hunting, to meet people from professions as diverse as stonemasonry and household moving. Almost none of these hunting friends had anything to do with his work in the consumer electronics industry, yet they all had to deal with one of his own daily concerns: customer relations. Hearing about their problems and techniques allowed him to view his own from a different perspective and helped him define principles that he could test in his work. Ultimately, what began as a personal network of hunting partners became operationally and strategically valuable to this manager. The key was his ability to build inside-outside links for maximum leverage. But we've seen others who avoided networking, or failed at it, because they let interpersonal chemistry, not strategic needs, determine which relationships they cultivated.

Just Do It

The word "work" is part of networking, and it is not easy work, because it involves reaching outside the borders of a manager's comfort zone. How, then, can managers lessen the pain and increase the gain? The trick is to leverage the elements from each domain of networking into the others—to seek out personal contacts who can be objective, strategic counselors, for example, or to transform colleagues in adjacent functions into a constituency. Above all, many managers will need to change their attitudes about the legitimacy and necessity of networking.

Mind your mind-set

In our ongoing discussions with managers learning to improve their networking skills, we often hear, "That's all well and good, but I already have a day job." Others, like Jody, consider working through networks a way to rely on "whom you know" rather than "what you know"—a hypocritical, even unethical way to get things done. Whatever the reason, when aspiring leaders do not believe that networking is one of the most important requirements of their new jobs, they will not allocate enough time and effort to see it pay off.

The best solution we've seen to this trap is a good role model. Many times, what appears to be unpalatable or unproductive behavior takes on a new light when a person you respect does it well and ethically. For example, Gabriel Chenard, general manager for Europe of a group of consumer product brands, learned from the previous general manager how to take advantage of branch visits to solidify his relationships with employees and customers. Every flight and car trip became a venue for catching up and building relationships with the people who were accompanying him. Watching how much his boss got done on what would otherwise be downtime, Gabriel adopted the practice as a crucial part of his own management style. Networking effectively and ethically, like any other tacit skill, is a matter of judgment and intuition. We learn by observing and getting feedback from those for whom it's second nature.

Work from the outside in
One of the most daunting aspects of strategic networking is that there often seems to be no natural "excuse" for making contact with a more senior person outside one's function or business unit. It's difficult to build a relationship with anyone, let alone a senior executive, without a reason for interacting, like a common task or a shared purpose.

Some successful managers find common ground from the outside in—by, for instance, transposing a personal interest into the strategic domain. Linda Henderson is a good example. An investment banker responsible for a group of media industry clients, she always wondered how to connect to some of her senior colleagues who served other industries. She resolved to make time for an extracurricular passion—the theater—in a way that would enhance her business development activities. Four times a year, her secretary booked a buffet dinner at a downtown hotel and reserved a block of theater tickets. Key clients were invited. Through these events, Linda not only developed her own business but also learned about her clients' companies in a way that generated ideas for other parts of her firm, thus enabling her to engage with colleagues.

Other managers build outside-inside connections by using their functional interests or expertise. For example, communities of practice exist (or can easily be created on the Internet) in almost every area of business from brand management to Six Sigma to global strategy. Savvy managers reach out to kindred spirits outside their organizations to contribute and multiply their knowledge; the information they glean, in more cases than not, becomes the "hook" for making internal connections.

Re-allocate your time

If an aspiring leader has not yet mastered the art of delegation, he or she will find many reasons not to spend time networking. Participating in formal and informal meetings with people in other units takes time away from functional responsibilities and internal team affairs. Between the obvious payoff of a task accomplished and the ambiguous, often delayed rewards of networking, naive managers repeatedly choose the former. The less they practice networking, the less efficient at it they become, and the vicious cycle continues.

Henrik, the production manager and board member we described earlier, for example, did what he needed to do in order to prepare for board meetings but did not associate with fellow board members outside those formal events. As a result, he was frequently surprised when other board members raised issues at the heart of his role. In contrast, effective business leaders spend a lot of time every day gathering the information they need to meet their goals, relying on informal discussions with a lot of people who are not necessarily in charge of an issue or task. They network in order to obtain information continually, not just at formal meetings.

Ask and you shall receive

Many managers equate having a good network with having a large database of contacts, or attending high-profile professional conferences and events. In fact, we've seen people kick off a networking initiative by improving their record keeping or adopting a network management tool. But they falter at the next step—picking up the phone. Instead, they wait until they need something *badly*. The best networkers do exactly the opposite: They take every opportunity to give to, and receive from, the network, whether they need help or not.

A network lives and thrives only when it is used. A good way to begin is to make a simple request or take the initiative to connect two people who would benefit from meeting each other. Doing something—anything—gets the ball rolling and builds confidence that one does, in fact, have something to contribute.

Stick to it

It takes a while to reap the benefits of networking. We have seen many managers resolve to put networking at the top of their agendas, only to be derailed by the first crisis that comes along. One example is Harris Roberts, a regulatory affairs expert who realized he needed a broader network to achieve his goal of becoming a business unit manager. To force himself into what felt like an "unnatural act," Harris volunteered to be the liaison for his business school cohort's alumni network. But six months later, when a major new-drug approval process overwhelmed his calendar, Harris dropped all outside activities. Two years later, he found himself out of touch and still a functional manager. He failed to recognize that by not taking the time to attend industry conferences or compare notes with his peers, he was missing out on the strategic perspective and information that would make him a more attractive candidate for promotion.

Building a leadership network is less a matter of skill than of will. When first efforts do not bring quick rewards, some may simply conclude that networking isn't among their talents. But networking is not a talent; nor does it require a gregarious, extroverted personality. It is a skill, one that takes practice. We have seen over and over again that people who work at networking can learn not only how to do it well but also how to enjoy it. And they tend to be more successful in their careers than those who fail to leverage external ties or insist on defining their jobs narrowly.

Making a successful leadership transition requires a shift from the confines of a clearly defined operational network. Aspiring leaders must learn to build and use strategic networks that cross organizational and functional boundaries, and then link them up in novel and innovative ways. It is a challenge to make the leap from a lifetime of functional contributions and hands-on control to the ambiguous process of building and working through networks. Leaders must find new ways of defining themselves and develop new relationships to anchor and feed their emerging personas. They must also accept that networking is one of the most important requirements of their new leadership roles and continue to allocate enough time and effort to see it pay off.

Originally published in January 2007. Reprint 1727

Management Time: Who's Got the Monkey?

by William Oncken, Jr., and Donald L. Wass

Editor's Note: This article was originally published in the November–December 1974 issue of HBR *and has been one of the publication's best-selling reprints. For its reissue,* Harvard Business Review *asked Stephen R. Covey to provide a commentary.*

WHY IS IT THAT MANAGERS are typically running out of time while their subordinates are typically running out of work? Here we shall explore the meaning of management time as it relates to the interaction between managers and their bosses, their peers, and their subordinates.

Specifically, we shall deal with three kinds of management time:

Boss-imposed time—used to accomplish those activities that the boss requires and that the manager cannot disregard without direct and swift penalty.

System-imposed time—used to accommodate requests from peers for active support. Neglecting these requests will also result in penalties, though not always as direct or swift.

Self-imposed time—used to do those things that the manager originates or agrees to do. A certain portion of this kind of time, however, will be taken by subordinates and is called *subordinate-imposed time*. The remaining portion will be the manager's own and is called *discretionary time*. Self-imposed time is not subject to penalty since neither the boss nor the system can discipline the manager for not doing what they didn't know he had intended to do in the first place.

To accommodate those demands, managers need to control the timing and the content of what they do. Since what their bosses and the system impose on them are subject to penalty, managers cannot tamper with those requirements. Thus their self-imposed time becomes their major area of concern.

Managers should try to increase the discretionary component of their self-imposed time by minimizing or doing away with the subordinate component. They will then use the added increment to get better control over their boss-imposed and system-imposed activities. Most managers spend much more time dealing with subordinates' problems than they even faintly realize. Hence we shall use the monkey-on-the-back metaphor to examine how subordinate-imposed time comes into being and what the superior can do about it.

Where Is the Monkey?

Let us imagine that a manager is walking down the hall and that he notices one of his subordinates, Jones, coming his way. When the two meet, Jones greets the manager with, "Good morning. By the way, we've got a problem. You see. . . ." As Jones continues, the manager recognizes in this problem the two characteristics common to all the problems his subordinates gratuitously bring to his attention. Namely, the manager knows (a) enough to get involved, but (b) not enough to make the on-the-spot decision expected of him. Eventually, the manager says, "So glad you brought this up. I'm in a rush right now. Meanwhile, let me think about it, and I'll let you know." Then he and Jones part company.

Let us analyze what just happened. Before the two of them met, on whose back was the "monkey"? The subordinate's. After they

Idea in Brief

You're racing down the hall. An employee stops you and says, "We've got a problem." You assume you should get involved but can't make an on-the-spot decision. You say, "Let me think about it."

You've just allowed a "monkey" to leap from your subordinate's back to yours. *You're* now working for your *subordinate*. Take on enough monkeys, and you won't have time to handle your *real* job: fulfilling your own boss's mandates and helping peers generate business results.

How to avoid accumulating monkeys? Develop your subordinates' initiative, say Oncken and Wass. For example, when an employee tries to hand you a problem, clarify whether he should: recommend and implement a solution, take action then brief you immediately, or act and report the outcome at a regular update.

When you encourage employees to handle their own monkeys, they acquire new skills—and you liberate time to do your own job.

parted, on whose back was it? The manager's. Subordinate-imposed time begins the moment a monkey successfully leaps from the back of a subordinate to the back of his or her superior and does not end until the monkey is returned to its proper owner for care and feeding. In accepting the monkey, the manager has voluntarily assumed a position subordinate to his subordinate. That is, he has allowed Jones to make him or her subordinate by doing two things a subordinate is generally expected to do for a boss—the manager has accepted a responsibility from his subordinate, and the manager has promised her a progress report.

The subordinate, to make sure the manager does not miss this point, will later stick her head in the manager's office and cheerily query, "How's it coming?" (This is called supervision.)

Or let us imagine in concluding a conference with Johnson, another subordinate, the manager's parting words are, "Fine. Send me a memo on that."

Let us analyze this one. The monkey is now on the subordinate's back because the next move is his, but it is poised for a leap. Watch that monkey. Johnson dutifully writes the requested memo and drops it in his out-basket. Shortly thereafter, the manager plucks it from his in-basket and reads it. Whose move is it now?

Idea in Practice

How to return monkeys to their proper owners? Oncken, Wass, and Steven Covey (in an afterword to this classic article) offer these suggestions.

Make Appointments to Deal with Monkeys

Avoid discussing any monkey on an ad hoc basis—for example, when you pass a subordinate in the hallway. You won't convey the proper seriousness. Instead, schedule an appointment to discuss the issue.

Specify Level of Initiative

Your employees can exercise five levels of initiative in handling on-the-job problems. From lowest to highest, the levels are:

1. Wait until told what to do.

2. Ask what to do.

3. Recommend an action, then with your approval, implement it.

4. Take independent action but advise you at once.

5. Take independent action and update you through routine procedure.

When an employee brings a problem to you, outlaw use of level 1 or 2. Agree on and assign level 3, 4, or 5 to the monkey. Take no more than 15 minutes to discuss the problem.

Agree on a Status Update

After deciding how to proceed, agree on a time and place when the employee will give you a progress report.

Examine Your Own Motives

Some managers secretly worry that if they encourage subordinates to take more initiative, they'll appear less strong, more vulnerable, and less useful. Instead, cultivate an inward sense of security that frees you to relinquish direct control and support employees' growth.

Develop Employees' Skills

Employees try to hand off monkeys when they lack the desire or ability to handle them. Help employees develop needed problem-solving skills. It's initially more time consuming than tackling problems yourself—but it saves time in the long run.

Foster Trust

Developing employees' initiative requires a trusting relationship between you and your subordinates. If they're afraid of failing, they'll keep bringing their monkeys to you rather than working to solve their own problems. To promote trust, reassure them it's safe to make mistakes.

The manager's. If he does not make that move soon, he will get a follow-up memo from the subordinate. (This is another form of supervision.) The longer the manager delays, the more frustrated the subordinate will become (he'll be spinning his wheels) and the more guilty the manager will feel (his backlog of subordinate-imposed time will be mounting).

Or suppose once again that at a meeting with a third subordinate, Smith, the manager agrees to provide all the necessary backing for a public relations proposal he has just asked Smith to develop. The manager's parting words to her are, "Just let me know how I can help."

Now let us analyze this. Again the monkey is initially on the subordinate's back. But for how long? Smith realizes that she cannot let the manager "know" until her proposal has the manager's approval. And from experience, she also realizes that her proposal will likely be sitting in the manager's briefcase for weeks before he eventually gets to it. Who's really got the monkey? Who will be checking up on whom? Wheel spinning and bottlenecking are well on their way again.

A fourth subordinate, Reed, has just been transferred from another part of the company so that he can launch and eventually manage a newly created business venture. The manager has said they should get together soon to hammer out a set of objectives for the new job, adding, "I will draw up an initial draft for discussion with you."

Let us analyze this one, too. The subordinate has the new job (by formal assignment) and the full responsibility (by formal delegation), but the manager has the next move. Until he makes it, he will have the monkey, and the subordinate will be immobilized.

Why does all of this happen? Because in each instance the manager and the subordinate assume at the outset, wittingly or unwittingly, that the matter under consideration is a joint problem. The monkey in each case begins its career astride both their backs. All it has to do is move the wrong leg, and—presto!—the subordinate deftly disappears. The manager is thus left with another acquisition for his menagerie. Of course, monkeys can be trained not to move the wrong leg. But it is easier to prevent them from straddling backs in the first place.

Who Is Working for Whom?

Let us suppose that these same four subordinates are so thoughtful and considerate of their superior's time that they take pains to allow no more than three monkeys to leap from each of their backs to his in any one day. In a five-day week, the manager will have picked up 60 screaming monkeys—far too many to do anything about them individually. So he spends his subordinate-imposed time juggling his "priorities."

Late Friday afternoon, the manager is in his office with the door closed for privacy so he can contemplate the situation, while his subordinates are waiting outside to get their last chance before the weekend to remind him that he will have to "fish or cut bait." Imagine what they are saying to one another about the manager as they wait: "What a bottleneck. He just can't make up his mind. How anyone ever got that high up in our company without being able to make a decision we'll never know."

Worst of all, the reason the manager cannot make any of these "next moves" is that his time is almost entirely eaten up by meeting his own boss-imposed and system-imposed requirements. To control those tasks, he needs discretionary time that is in turn denied him when he is preoccupied with all these monkeys. The manager is caught in a vicious circle. But time is a-wasting (an understatement). The manager calls his secretary on the intercom and instructs her to tell his subordinates that he won't be able to see them until Monday morning. At 7 PM, he drives home, intending with firm resolve to return to the office tomorrow to get caught up over the weekend. He returns bright and early the next day only to see, on the nearest green of the golf course across from his office window, a foursome. Guess who?

That does it. He now knows who is really working for whom. Moreover, he now sees that if he actually accomplishes during this weekend what he came to accomplish, his subordinates' morale will go up so sharply that they will each raise the limit on the number of monkeys they will let jump from their backs to his. In short, he now sees, with the clarity of a revelation on a mountaintop, that the more he gets caught up, the more he will fall behind.

He leaves the office with the speed of a person running away from a plague. His plan? To get caught up on something else he hasn't had time for in years: a weekend with his family. (This is one of the many varieties of discretionary time.)

Sunday night he enjoys ten hours of sweet, untroubled slumber, because he has clear-cut plans for Monday. He is going to get rid of his subordinate-imposed time. In exchange, he will get an equal amount of discretionary time, part of which he will spend with his subordinates to make sure that they learn the difficult but rewarding managerial art called "The Care and Feeding of Monkeys."

The manager will also have plenty of discretionary time left over for getting control of the timing and the content not only of his boss-imposed time but also of his system-imposed time. It may take months, but compared with the way things have been, the rewards will be enormous. His ultimate objective is to manage his time.

Getting Rid of the Monkeys

The manager returns to the office Monday morning just late enough so that his four subordinates have collected outside his office waiting to see him about their monkeys. He calls them in one by one. The purpose of each interview is to take a monkey, place it on the desk between them, and figure out together how the next move might conceivably be the subordinate's. For certain monkeys, that will take some doing. The subordinate's next move may be so elusive that the manager may decide—just for now—merely to let the monkey sleep on the subordinate's back overnight and have him or her return with it at an appointed time the next morning to continue the joint quest for a more substantive move by the subordinate. (Monkeys sleep just as soundly overnight on subordinates' backs as they do on superiors'.)

As each subordinate leaves the office, the manager is rewarded by the sight of a monkey leaving his office on the subordinate's back.

Making Time for Gorillas

by Stephen R. Covey

WHEN BILL ONCKEN WROTE this article in 1974, managers were in a terrible bind. They were desperate for a way to free up their time, but command and control was the status quo. Managers felt they weren't allowed to empower their subordinates to make decisions. Too dangerous. Too risky. That's why Oncken's message—give the monkey back to its rightful owner—involved a critically important paradigm shift. Many managers working today owe him a debt of gratitude.

It is something of an understatement, however, to observe that much has changed since Oncken's radical recommendation. Command and control as a management philosophy is all but dead, and "empowerment" is the word of the day in most organizations trying to thrive in global, intensely competitive markets. But command and control stubbornly remains a common practice. Management thinkers and executives have discovered in the last decade that bosses cannot just give a monkey back to their subordinates and then merrily get on with their own business. Empowering subordinates is hard and complicated work.

The reason: when you give problems back to subordinates to solve themselves, you have to be sure that they have both the desire and the ability to do so. As every executive knows, that isn't always the case. Enter a whole new set of problems. Empowerment often means you have to develop people, which is initially much more time consuming than solving the problem on your own.

Just as important, empowerment can only thrive when the whole organization buys into it—when formal systems and the informal culture support it. Managers need to be rewarded for delegating decisions and developing people. Otherwise, the degree of real empowerment in an organization will vary according to the beliefs and practices of individual managers.

But perhaps the most important lesson about empowerment is that effective delegation—the kind Oncken advocated—depends on a trusting relationship between a manager and his subordinate. Oncken's message may have been ahead of his time, but what he suggested was still a fairly dictatorial solution. He basically told bosses, "Give the problem back!" Today, we know that this approach by itself is too authoritarian. To delegate effectively, executives need to establish a running dialogue with subordinates. They need to establish a partnership. After all, if subordinates are afraid of failing in front of their boss, they'll keep coming back for help rather than truly take initiative.

Oncken's article also doesn't address an aspect of delegation that has greatly interested me during the past two decades—that many managers are actually *eager* to take on their subordinates' monkeys. Nearly all the managers I talk with agree that their people are underutilized in their present jobs. But even some of the most successful, seemingly self-assured executives have talked about how hard it is to give up control to their subordinates.

I've come to attribute that eagerness for control to a common, deep-seated belief that rewards in life are scarce and fragile. Whether they learn it from their family, school, or athletics, many people establish an identity by comparing themselves with others. When they see others gain power, information, money, or recognition, for instance, they experience what the psychologist Abraham Maslow called "a feeling of deficiency"—a sense that something is being taken from them. That makes it hard for them to be genuinely happy about the success of others—even of their loved ones. Oncken implies that managers can easily give back or refuse monkeys, but many managers may subconsciously fear that a subordinate taking the initiative will make them appear a little less strong and a little more vulnerable.

How, then, do managers develop the inward security, the mentality of "abundance," that would enable them to relinquish control and seek the growth and development of those around them? The work I've done with numerous organizations suggests that managers who live with integrity according to a principle-based value system are most likely to sustain an empowering style of leadership.

Given the times in which he wrote, it was no wonder that Oncken's message resonated with managers. But it was reinforced by Oncken's wonderful gift for storytelling. I got to know Oncken on the speaker's circuit in the 1970s, and I was always impressed by how he dramatized his ideas in colorful detail. Like the Dilbert comic strip, Oncken had a tongue-in-cheek style that got to the core of managers' frustrations and made them want to take back control of their time. And the monkey on your back wasn't just a metaphor for Oncken—it was his personal symbol. I saw him several times walking through airports with a stuffed monkey on his shoulder.

I'm not surprised that his article is one of the two best-selling HBR articles ever. Even with all we know about empowerment, its vivid message is even more important and relevant now than it was 25 years ago. Indeed, Oncken's insight is a basis for my own work on time management, in which I have

(continued)

people categorize their activities according to urgency and importance. I've heard from executives again and again that half or more of their time is spent on matters that are urgent but not important. They're trapped in an endless cycle of dealing with other people's monkeys, yet they're reluctant to help those people take their own initiative. As a result, they're often too busy to spend the time they need on the real gorillas in their organization. Oncken's article remains a powerful wake-up call for managers who need to delegate effectively.

Stephen R. Covey is vice chairman of the Franklin Covey Company, a global provider of leadership development and productivity services and products.

For the next 24 hours, the subordinate will not be waiting for the manager; instead, the manager will be waiting for the subordinate.

Later, as if to remind himself that there is no law against his engaging in a constructive exercise in the interim, the manager strolls by the subordinate's office, sticks his head in the door, and cheerily asks, "How's it coming?" (The time consumed in doing this is discretionary for the manager and boss imposed for the subordinate.)

When the subordinate (with the monkey on his or her back) and the manager meet at the appointed hour the next day, the manager explains the ground rules in words to this effect:

"At no time while I am helping you with this or any other problem will your problem become my problem. The instant your problem becomes mine, you no longer have a problem. I cannot help a person who hasn't got a problem.

"When this meeting is over, the problem will leave this office exactly the way it came in—on your back. You may ask my help at any appointed time, and we will make a joint determination of what the next move will be and which of us will make it.

"In those rare instances where the next move turns out to be mine, you and I will determine it together. I will not make any move alone."

The manager follows this same line of thought with each subordinate until about 11 AM, when he realizes that he doesn't have to close his door. His monkeys are gone. They will return—but by appointment only. His calendar will assure this.

Transferring the Initiative

What we have been driving at in this monkey-on-the-back analogy is that managers can transfer initiative back to their subordinates and keep it there. We have tried to highlight a truism as obvious as it is subtle: namely, before developing initiative in subordinates, the manager must see to it that they *have* the initiative. Once the manager takes it back, he will no longer have it and he can kiss his discretionary time good-bye. It will all revert to subordinate-imposed time.

Nor can the manager and the subordinate effectively have the same initiative at the same time. The opener, "Boss, we've got a problem," implies this duality and represents, as noted earlier, a monkey astride two backs, which is a very bad way to start a monkey on its career. Let us, therefore, take a few moments to examine what we call "The Anatomy of Managerial Initiative."

There are five degrees of initiative that the manager can exercise in relation to the boss and to the system:

1. wait until told (lowest initiative);

2. ask what to do;

3. recommend, then take resulting action;

4. act, but advise at once;

5. and act on own, then routinely report (highest initiative).

Clearly, the manager should be professional enough not to indulge in initiatives 1 and 2 in relation either to the boss or to the system. A manager who uses initiative 1 has no control over either the timing or the content of boss-imposed or system-imposed time and thereby forfeits any right to complain about what he or she is told to do or when. The manager who uses initiative 2 has control over the timing but not over the content. Initiatives 3, 4, and 5 leave the manager in control of both, with the greatest amount of control being exercised at level 5.

In relation to subordinates, the manager's job is twofold. First, to outlaw the use of initiatives 1 and 2, thus giving subordinates no choice but to learn and master "Completed Staff Work." Second, to see that for each problem leaving his or her office there is an agreed-upon level of initiative assigned to it, in addition to an agreed-upon time and place for the next manager-subordinate conference. The latter should be duly noted on the manager's calendar.

The Care and Feeding of Monkeys

To further clarify our analogy between the monkey on the back and the processes of assigning and controlling, we shall refer briefly to the manager's appointment schedule, which calls for five hard-and-fast rules governing the "Care and Feeding of Monkeys." (Violation of these rules will cost discretionary time.)

Rule 1
Monkeys should be fed or shot. Otherwise, they will starve to death, and the manager will waste valuable time on postmortems or attempted resurrections.

Rule 2
The monkey population should be kept below the maximum number the manager has time to feed. Subordinates will find time to work as many monkeys as he or she finds time to feed, but no more. It shouldn't take more than five to 15 minutes to feed a properly maintained monkey.

Rule 3
Monkeys should be fed by appointment only. The manager should not have to hunt down starving monkeys and feed them on a catch-as-catch-can basis.

Rule 4

Monkeys should be fed face-to-face or by telephone, but never by mail. (Remember—with mail, the next move will be the manager's.) Documentation may add to the feeding process, but it cannot take the place of feeding.

Rule 5

Every monkey should have an assigned next feeding time and degree of initiative. These may be revised at any time by mutual consent but never allowed to become vague or indefinite. Otherwise, the monkey will either starve to death or wind up on the manager's back.

"Get control over the timing and content of what you do" is appropriate advice for managing time. The first order of business is for the manager to enlarge his or her discretionary time by eliminating subordinate-imposed time. The second is for the manager to use a portion of this newfound discretionary time to see to it that each subordinate actually has the initiative and applies it. The third is for the manager to use another portion of the increased discretionary time to get and keep control of the timing and content of both boss-imposed and system-imposed time. All these steps will increase the manager's leverage and enable the value of each hour spent in managing management time to multiply without theoretical limit.

Originally published in November 1999. Reprint 99609

How Managers
Become Leaders

The seven seismic shifts of perspective
and responsibility. *by Michael D. Watkins*

HARALD (NOT HIS REAL NAME) is a high-potential leader with 15 years of experience at a leading European chemical company. He started as an assistant product manager in the plastics unit and was quickly transferred to Hong Kong to help set up the unit's new Asian business center. As sales there soared, he soon won a promotion to sales manager. Three years later he returned to Europe as the marketing and sales director for Europe, the Middle East, and Africa, overseeing a group of 80 professionals. Continuing his string of successes, he was promoted to vice president of marketing and sales for the polyethylene division, responsible for several lines of products, related services, and a staff of nearly 200.

All of Harald's hard work culminated in his appointment as the head of the company's plastic resins unit, a business with more than 3,000 employees worldwide. Quite intentionally, the company had assigned him to run a small but thriving business with a strong team. The idea was to give him the opportunity to move beyond managing sales and marketing, get his arms around an entire business, learn what it meant to head up a unit with the help of his more-experienced team, and take his leadership skills to the next level in a situation free from complicating problems or crises. The setup seemed perfect, but a few months into the new position, Harald was struggling mightily.

Like Harald, many rising stars trip when they shift from leading a function to leading an enterprise and for the first time taking responsibility for a P&L and oversight of executives across corporate functions. It truly is different at the top. To find out how, I took an in-depth look at this critical turning point, conducting an extensive series of interviews with more than 40 executives, including managers who had developed high-potential talent, senior HR professionals, and individuals who had recently made the move to enterprise leadership for the first time.

What I found is that to make the transition successfully, executives must navigate a tricky set of changes in their leadership focus and skills, which I call the seven seismic shifts. They must learn to move from specialist to generalist, analyst to integrator, tactician to strategist, bricklayer to architect, problem solver to agenda setter, warrior to diplomat, and supporting cast member to lead role. Like so many of his peers, Harald had trouble negotiating most of these shifts. To see what makes them so difficult, let's follow him through each of them, as he confronts unnerving surprises, makes unwarranted assumptions, encounters entirely new demands on his time and imagination, makes decisions in ignorance, and learns from his mistakes.

Specialist to Generalist

Harald's immediate challenge was shifting from leading a single function to overseeing the full set of business functions. In his first couple of months, this shift left him feeling disoriented and less confident in his ability to make good judgments. And so he fell into a classic trap—overmanaging the function he knew well and undermanaging the others. Fortunately for Harald, this became crystal clear when his vice president of HR gave him some blunt feedback about his relationship with his sales and marketing VP: "You are driving Claire crazy. You need to give her some space."

Harald's tendency to stay in his functional comfort zone is an understandable reaction to the stresses of moving up to a much broader role. It would be wonderful if newly appointed enterprise leaders

Idea in Brief

Few leadership transitions are as challenging as the move from running a function to running an entire enterprise for the first time.

The scope and complexity of the job dramatically increase in ways that can leave newly minted unit heads feeling overwhelmed and uncertain. The skills that they've honed in their previous roles—mastery of their function, organizational know-how, the ability to build and motivate a team—are no longer enough. For the first time, these executives must transform themselves into generalists who understand all the functions. They must learn to hire, judge, and mediate with a far wider variety of people. They must confront a whole new range of tough questions: What are the big issues on our corporate agenda? What opportunities and threats does the whole business face? How can I ensure the success of the entire organization?

At this critical turning point, executives must undergo seven seismic shifts—a tricky set of changes in their leadership focus that require them to develop new skills and conceptual frameworks.

were world-class experts in all business functions, but of course they never are. In some instances they have gained experience by rotating through various functions or working on cross-functional projects, which certainly helps. (See the sidebar "How to Develop Strong Enterprise Leaders.") But the reality is that the move to enterprise leadership always requires executives who've been specialists to quickly turn into generalists who know enough about all the functions to run their businesses.

What is "enough"? Enterprise leaders must be able to (1) make decisions that are good for the business as a whole and (2) evaluate the talent on their teams. To do both they need to recognize that business functions are distinct managerial subcultures, each with its own mental models and language. Effective leaders understand the different ways that professionals in finance, marketing, operations, HR, and R&D approach business problems, and the various tools (discounted cash flow, customer segmentation, process flow, succession planning, stage gates, and the like) that each discipline applies. Leaders must be able to speak the language of all the functions and translate for them when necessary. And critically, leaders must

The Seven Seismic Shifts

ALL THE SHIFTS A FUNCTION head must make when first becoming an enterprise leader involve learning new skills and cultivating new mindsets. Here are the shifts and what each requires executives to do:

Specialist to Generalist

Understand the mental models, tools, and terms used in key business functions and develop templates for evaluating the leaders of those functions.

Analyst to Integrator

Integrate the collective knowledge of cross-functional teams and make appropriate trade-offs to solve complex organizational problems.

Tactician to Strategist

Shift fluidly between the details and the larger picture, perceive important patterns in complex environments, and anticipate and influence the reactions of key external players.

Bricklayer to Architect

Understand how to analyze and design organizational systems so that strategy, structure, operating models, and skill bases fit together effectively and

know the right questions to ask and the right metrics for evaluating and recruiting people to manage areas in which they themselves are not experts.

The good news for Harald was that, in addition to assigning him to a high-performing unit, his company had strong systems in place for evaluating and developing talent in key functions. These included well-crafted systems for performance reviews and 360-degree feedback, and for collecting input from corporate functions. His heads of finance and HR, for instance, while reporting directly to him, also had dotted-line reporting relationships with their respective corporate departments, which assisted Harald with their evaluation and development. So he had plenty of resources to help him understand what "excellence" meant for each function.

efficiently, and harness this understanding to make needed organizational changes.

Problem Solver to Agenda Setter

Define the problems the organization should focus on, and spot issues that don't fall neatly into any one function but are still important.

Warrior to Diplomat

Proactively shape the environment in which the business operates by influencing key external constituencies, including the government, NGOs, the media, and investors.

Supporting Cast Member to Lead Role

Exhibit the right behaviors as a role model for the organization and learn to communicate with and inspire large groups of people both directly and, increasingly, indirectly.

By investing directly in creating standardized evaluation schemes for each function, companies can ensure that new enterprise leaders get the lay of the land faster. But even if their firms don't have such systems, aspiring enterprise leaders can prepare themselves by building relationships with colleagues in other functions, seeking to learn from them (perhaps in exchange for insight into their own functions) so that they can develop their own templates.

Analyst to Integrator

The primary responsibility of functional leaders is to recruit, develop, and manage people who focus in analytical depth on specific business activities. An enterprise leader's job is to manage and integrate the collective knowledge of those functional teams to solve important organizational problems.

Harald found himself struggling with this shift early on as he sought to address the many competing demands of the business. His sales and marketing VP, for example, wanted to aggressively go to market with a new product, while his head of operations worried that production couldn't be ramped up quickly enough to meet the sales staff's demand scenarios. Harald's team expected him to balance the needs of the supply side of the business (operations) with those of its demand side (sales and marketing), to know when to focus on the quarterly business results (finance) and when to invest in the future (R&D), to decide how much attention to devote to execution and how much to innovation, and to make many other such calls.

Once again, executives need general knowledge of the various functions to resolve such competing issues, but that isn't enough. The skills required have less to do with analysis and more to do with understanding how to make trade-offs and explain the rationale for those decisions. Here, too, previous experience with cross-functional or new-product development teams would stand newly minted enterprise leaders in good stead, as would a previous apprenticeship as a chief of staff to a senior executive. But ultimately, as Harald found, there is no substitute for actually making the calls and learning from their outcome.

Tactician to Strategist

In his early months, Harald threw himself into the myriad details of the business. Being tactical was seductive—the activities were so concrete and the results so immediate. Consequently, he lost himself in the day-to-day flow of attending meetings, making decisions, and pushing projects forward.

The problem with this, of course, was that a core part of Harald's new role was to be strategist-in-chief for the unit he now led. To do that, he had to let go of many of the details and free his mind and his time to focus on higher-level matters. More generally, he needed to adopt a strategic mind-set.

How do tactically strong leaders learn to develop such a mind-set? By cultivating three skills: level shifting, pattern recognition, and mental simulation. *Level shifting* is the ability to move fluidly among levels of analysis—to know when to focus on the details, when to focus on the big picture, and how the two relate. *Pattern recognition* is the ability to discern important causal relationships and other significant patterns in a complex business and its environment—that is, to separate the signal from the noise. *Mental simulation* is the ability to anticipate how outside parties (competitors, regulators, the media, key members of the public) will respond to what you do, to predict their actions and reactions in order to define the best course to take. In Harald's first year, for instance, an Asian competitor introduced a lower-cost substitute for a key resin product his unit made. Harald needed not only to consider the immediate threat but also to think expansively about what the competitor's future intentions might be. Was the Asian company going to use this low-end product to forge strong customer relationships and progressively offer a broader range of products? If so, what options should Harald's unit pursue? How would the competitor respond to what Harald chose to do? Those were not questions he had been responsible for as head of marketing and sales. In the end, after analyzing various courses of action with his senior team, he chose to lower prices, forgoing some current profits in an effort to slow the loss of market share—a move he did not live to regret.

Are strategic thinkers born or made? The answer is both. There's no doubt that strategic thinking, like any other skill, can be improved with training. But the ability to shift through different levels of analysis, recognize patterns, and construct mental models requires some natural propensity. One of the paradoxes of leadership development is that people earn promotions to senior functional levels predominantly by being good at blocking and tackling, but employees with strategic talent may struggle at lower levels because they focus less on the details. Darwinian forces can winnow strategic thinkers out of the developmental pipeline too soon if companies don't adopt explicit policies to identify and to some degree protect them in their early careers.

How to Develop Strong Enterprise Leaders

Early in their careers, give potential leaders . . .

- Experience on cross-functional projects and then responsibility for them
- An international assignment (if it's a global business)
- Exposure to a broad range of business situations: startup, accelerated growth, sustaining success, realignment, turnaround, and shutdown

When their leadership promise becomes evident, give high potentials . . .

- A position on a senior management team
- Experience with external stakeholders (investors, the media, key customers)
- An assignment as chief of staff for an experienced enterprise leader

Bricklayer to Architect

Too often, senior executives dabble in the profession of organizational design without a license—and end up committing malpractice. They come into their first enterprise-level role itching to make their mark and then target elements of the organization that seem relatively easy to change, like strategy or structure, without completely understanding the effect their moves will have on the organization as a whole.

About four months into his new role, for example, Harald concluded that he needed to restructure the business to focus more on customers and less on product lines. It was natural for him, as a former head of sales and marketing, to think this way. In his eyes it was obvious that the business was too rooted in product development and operations and that its structure was an outdated legacy of the way the unit had been founded and grown. So he was surprised when his restructuring proposal was met first with stunned silence from his team and then with vociferous opposition. It rapidly became clear that the existing structure in this successful division was linked in intricate and nonobvious ways to its key processes

- An appointment to lead an acquisition integration or a substantial restructuring

Some time just before their first enterprise promotion, send rising stars . . .

- To a substantial executive program that addresses such capabilities as organizational design, business process improvement, and transition management, and allows them to build external networks

At the time of their first enterprise-level promotion, place new enterprise leaders in units that are . . .

- Small, distinct, and thriving

- Staffed with an experienced and assertive team that they can learn from

and talent bases. To sell the company's chemicals, for instance, the salespeople needed to have deep product knowledge and the ability to consult with customers on applications. A shift to a customer-focused approach would have required them to sell a broader range of complex products and acquire huge amounts of new expertise. So while a move to a customer-focused structure had potential benefits, certain trade-offs needed to be evaluated. Implementation would, for instance, require significant adjustments to processes and substantial investments in employee retraining. These changes demanded a great deal of thought and analysis.

As leaders move up to the enterprise level, they become responsible for designing and altering the architecture of their organization—its strategy, structure, processes, and skill bases. To be effective organizational architects, they need to think in terms of systems. They must understand how the key elements of the organization fit together and not naively believe, as Harald once did, that they can alter one element without thinking through the implications for all the others. Harald learned this the hard way because nothing in his experience as a functional leader had afforded him the opportunity to think about an organization as a system. Nor did he have enough experience with large-scale organizational change to develop those insights from observation.

In this Harald was typical: Enterprise leaders need to know the principles of organizational change and change management, including the mechanics of organizational design, business process improvement, and transition management. Yet few rising executives get any formal training in these domains, leaving most of them ill equipped to be the architects of their organizations—or even to be educated consumers of the work of organizational development professionals. Here Harald was once again fortunate in having—and having the sense to rely on—an experienced staff that offered him cogent advice about the many interdependencies he had not originally considered. Not all new enterprise leaders are that lucky, of course. But if their companies have invested in sending them to executive education programs that teach organizational change, they'll be better prepared for this shift.

Problem Solver to Agenda Setter

Many managers are promoted to senior levels on the strength of their ability to fix problems. When they become enterprise leaders, however, they must focus less on solving problems and more on defining which problems the organization should be tackling.

To do that, Harald had to perceive the full range of opportunities and threats facing his business, and focus the attention of his team on only the most important ones. He also had to identify the "white spaces"—issues that don't fall neatly into any one function but are still important to the business, such as diversity.

The number of concerns Harald now had to consider was headspinning. When he had run sales and marketing, he had gained some appreciation for how difficult it was for business heads to prioritize all the issues thrown at them in any given day, week, or month. Still, he was surprised by the scope and complexity of some of the problems at this level. He wasn't sure how to allocate his time and immediately felt overloaded. He knew he needed to delegate more, but he wasn't clear yet about which tasks and assignments he could safely leave to others.

How Do I Evaluate a Sales Executive?

ENTERPRISE LEADERS NEED TO EVALUATE the work of all their functional executives, not just those in the same area they came from. A simple template that systematically lists the most important metrics to track for a particular function, as well as which ones indicate trouble is brewing, will help new leaders get up to speed. Here is an example of a template for sales:

Core Performance Metrics

- Sales of key products versus competitors' key products
- Market share growth in key products
- Execution against business plan commitments

People Management Metrics

- Vacancy rate by region or district
- Rate of internal promotions and strength of internal succession pipeline
- Number of regrettable employee losses and the reasons for them
- Success in recruiting and selection

Customer Metrics

- Customer satisfaction and retention rates
- Evidence of understanding purchasing patterns
- Average amount of sales person interaction with customers

Warning Signs

- Regrettable losses of sales personnel
- Flattening or declining sales
- Lack of internal development for future sales leaders
- Internal promotions with poor results
- Inability to communicate product advantages and disadvantages
- Poor assessment of the organization's strengths and weaknesses
- Lack of time in the field or interactions with customers
- Lack of partnering skills with marketing and other key functions

The skills he had honed as a functional leader—mastery of sales and marketing tools and techniques, organizational know-how, and even the ability to mobilize talent and promote teamwork—were not enough. To work out which problems his team should focus on—that is, to set the agenda—he had to learn to navigate a far more uncertain and ambiguous environment than he was used to. He also needed to learn to communicate priorities in ways his organization could respond to. Given his sales and marketing background, Harald struggled less with how to communicate his agenda. The challenge was figuring out what that agenda was. To some degree he just had to learn from experience, but here again he was aided by the members of his team, who pressed him for guidance on issues they knew he needed to consider. He also could rely on the company's annual planning process, which provided a structure for defining key goals for his unit.

Warrior to Diplomat

In his previous roles, Harald had focused primarily on marshaling the troops to defeat the competition. Now he found himself devoting a surprising amount of time to influencing a host of external constituencies, including regulators, the media, investors, and NGOs. His support staff was bombarded with requests for his time: Could he participate in industry or government forums sponsored by the government affairs department? Would he be willing to sit for an interview with an editor from a leading business publication? Could he meet with a key group of institutional investors? Some of these groups he was familiar with; others not at all. But what was entirely new to him was his responsibility not just to interact with various stakeholders but also to proactively address their concerns in ways that meshed with the firm's interests. Little of Harald's previous experience prepared him for the challenges of being a corporate diplomat.

What do effective corporate diplomats do? They use the tools of diplomacy—negotiation, persuasion, conflict management, and alliance building—to shape the external business environment to support their strategic objectives. In the process they often find themselves collaborating with people with whom they compete aggressively in the market every day.

To do this well, enterprise leaders need to embrace a new mind-set—to look for ways that interests can or do align, understand how decisions are made in different kinds of organizations, and develop effective strategies for influencing others. They must also understand how to recruit and manage employees of a kind that they have probably never supervised before: professionals in key supporting functions such as government relations and corporate communications. And they must recognize that these employees' initiatives have longer horizons than the ongoing business, with its focus on quarterly or even annual results, does. Initiatives like a campaign to shape the development of government regulation can take years to unfold. It took Harald a while to understand this, as his staffers educated him about how painstakingly they managed issues over protracted periods of time and how they periodically bemoaned the results when someone took his eye off the ball.

Supporting Cast Member to Lead Role

Finally, becoming an enterprise leader means moving to center stage under the bright lights. The intensity of the attention and the almost constant need to keep up his guard caught Harald by surprise. He was somewhat shocked to discover how much stock people placed in what he said and did. Not long after he first took the job, for example, he met with his vice president of R&D and mused about a new way of packaging an existing product. Two weeks later a preliminary feasibility report for it appeared on his desk.

In part, this shift is about having a much greater impact as a role model. Managers at all levels are role models to some degree. But at the enterprise level, their influence is magnified, as everyone looks to them for vision, inspiration, and cues about the "right" behaviors and attitudes. For good or ill, the personal styles and quirks of senior leaders are infectious, whether they are observed directly by employees or indirectly transmitted from their reports to the level below and on down through the organization. This effect can't really be avoided, but enterprise leaders can make it less inadvertent by cultivating more self-awareness and taking the time to develop empathy with subordinates' viewpoints. After all, it wasn't so long ago that they were the subordinates, drawing these kinds of inferences from their own bosses' behavior.

Then there is the question of what it means, practically speaking, to lead large groups of people—how to define a compelling vision and share it in an inspiring way. Harald, already a strong communicator who was used to selling ideas along with products, still needed to adjust his thinking in this regard (though perhaps less so than some of his counterparts). In his previous job he had maintained a reasonable degree of personal, albeit sometimes sporadic, contact with most of his employees. Now that he was overseeing 3,000-plus people scattered around the globe, that was simply impossible.

The implications of this became clear as he worked with his team to craft the annual strategy. When the time came to communicate it to the organization, he realized that he couldn't simply go out and sell it himself; he had to work more through his direct reports and find other channels, such as video, for spreading the word. And after touring most of the unit's facilities, Harald likewise worried that he'd never really be able to figure out what was happening on the front lines. So rather than meet just with leaders when he made site visits, he instituted brown-bag lunches with small groups of frontline employees and tuned in to online discussion groups in which employees could comment on the company.

FOR THE MOST PART, the seven shifts involve switching from left-brain, analytical thinking to right-brain conceptual mind-sets. But that doesn't mean enterprise leaders never spend time on tactics or on functional concerns. It's just that they spend far, far less time on those responsibilities than they used to in their previous roles. In fact, it's often helpful for enterprise leaders to engage someone else—a chief of staff, a chief operating officer, or a project manager— to focus on execution, as a way to free up time for their new role.

As for Harald, his story ended well. He was fortunate to be working for a company that believed in leadership development and to have an experienced team that was able—and willing—to give him effective counsel. So despite the many bumps in the road, the business continued to thrive, and Harald eventually found his stride as an enterprise leader. Three years later, armed with all this experience, he was asked to take over a much larger, struggling unit of the company and initiated a successful turn-around. Reflecting back, he says, "The skills that got you where you are may not be the requisite skills to get you to where you need to go. This doesn't discount the accomplishments of your past, but they will not be everything you need for the next leg of the journey."

Originally published in June 2012. Reprint R1206C

ROBERT B. CIALDINI is the president of Influence at Work and a professor of psychology and marketing, emeritus, at Arizona State University.

JOHN J. GABARRO is the UPS Foundation Professor of Human Resource Management, Emeritus, at Harvard Business School.

DANIEL GOLEMAN cochairs the Consortium for Research on Emotional Intelligence in Organizations at Rutgers University. He is the coauthor of *Primal Leadership: Unleashing the Power of Emotional Intelligence* (Harvard Business Review Press, 2013).

LINDA A. HILL is the Wallace Brett Donham Professor Business Administration at Harvard Business School. She is the coauthor of *Being the Boss: The 3 Imperatives for Becoming a Great Leader* (Harvard Business Review Press, 2011).

MARK LEE HUNTER is an adjunct professor at INSEAD and a co-founder of the Stakeholder Media Project at the INSEAD Social Innovation Center.

HERMINIA IBARRA is the Cora Chaired Professor of Leadership and Learning and a professor of organizational behavior at INSEAD. She is the author of *Act Like a Leader, Think Like a Leader* (Harvard Business Review Press, 2015).

JOHN P. KOTTER is the Konosuke Matsushita Professor of Leadership, Emeritus, at Harvard Business School and the author of *Leading Change* (Harvard Business Review Press, 2012).

WILLIAM ONCKEN, JR., was chairman of the William Oncken Corporation, a management consulting company.

LAKSHMI RAMARAJAN is an assistant professor at Harvard Business School.

ERIN REID is an assistant professor at Boston University's Questrom School of Business.

CAROL A. WALKER is the president of Prepared to Lead, a management consulting firm in Boston. Before founding the company, she worked for 15 years as an executive in the insurance and technology industries.

DONALD L. WASS is head of the Dallas–Fort Worth region of The Executive Committee (TEC), an international organization for presidents and CEOs.

MICHAEL D. WATKINS is the chairman of Genesis Advisers, a professor at IMD, and the author of *The First 90 Days, Updated and Expanded* (Harvard Business Review Press, 2013).

Index

accepters, in high-intensity
    workplaces, 51–52, 57
achievement, 92–94
activities, vs. goals, 45–46
agenda setters, 169, 174, 176
agenda setting, 3–4
alignment, of team, 28–29
analysts, 168, 169–170
approachability, 105
architect, vs. bricklayer, 168,
    172–174
assessment, of current team, 20–26
authenticity
    adaptive approach to, 103
    leadership struggle with, 102–106
    multicultural environments
      and, 111
    paradox, 101–113
    playful frame of mind and,
      108–112
    training, 107
authority
    vs. approachability, 105
    of managers, 4, 7–12
    persuasion and, 62, 65, 72–75
    predispositions toward, 124–126
    undermining of, 43–44
autonomy, 7, 58–59

Best Buy, 50
big-picture thinking, 39, 44–46, 81
biological impulses, 89–90
boss(es)
    becoming the, 1–18
    compatible work style with, 118,
      122–123, 127–128
    decision making style of, 127–128
    getting help from, by new
      managers, 16–18, 38, 40–42
    information flow with, 129–130
    managing your, 115–131

mutual dependence and, 119–120,
    124
mutual expectations and, 128–129
relationship with, 119–120,
    123–131
self-understanding and, 123–126
understanding the, 120–123
use of time and resources of,
    118, 130–131
See also leaders; superiors
boss-imposed time, 151, 156
bricklayer, vs. architect, 168, 172–174

candor, 101
career advancement, 106
chameleons, 104, 110
change, initiation of, 14–16
change management, 174
character, 10
coaching, 5, 35–36, 44, 96, 142–143
cognitive skills, 81
comfort zone, 102, 166–167
command and control, 158–159
communication
    between boss and new managers,
      40–42
    cross-cultural, 96
competence, 10 11, 22, 36
competency models, 80–81
confidence, 38–39, 42–44
connectivity, 103
consistency, 65, 69–72
constructive feedback, 39, 46–48
control
    of direct reports, 4, 12–13
    See also command and control
counterdependent behavior,
    124–126
credibility, 10, 11, 13, 101
cross-cultural dialogue, 96
cross-functional projects, 172

183

decision making style, 127–128
delegation, 36–40, 147, 158–159, 174
dependability, 118, 130
difficult conversations, 47–48
diplomat, vs. warrior, 169, 176–177
direct reports. *See* employees;
  subordinates
discretionary time, 151–152,
  156–157
diverse role models, 109–110
drop-by meetings, 42
Drucker, Peter, 127

emergencies, responding to, 44–45
emotional intelligence, 79–99
  components of, 81, 82–84
  empathy and, 81, 83, 84, 86–87,
    94–97
  evaluating, 80–81, 85
  learning, 86–87
  motivation and, 81, 82, 84, 92–94
  performance and, 85
  self-awareness and, 81, 82, 84, 85,
    88–89
  self-regulation and, 81, 82, 84,
    89–92
  social skill and, 81, 83, 84, 97–99
  strengthening your, 83
emotional messages, 105–106
emotions, 89–90
empathy, 81, 83, 84, 86–87, 94–97
employees
  empowerment of, 158–159
  as ideal workers, 49–59
  minimizing time-based rewards
    for, 58–59
  personal lives of, 49–50, 52,
    56–59
  problems brought by, 151–163
  skill development in, 154
  See also subordinates

empowerment, 158–159
energy, 22
enterprise leadership, 165–179
ethics, 77–78
exclusive information, 65, 76
experimentation, 109
expertise, 73–74, 77
expert opinions, 72–73
external stakeholders, 172

feedback
  constructive, 39, 46–48
  negative, 106, 108
focus, 23
friendliness, 97
functional leaders, 169

generalists, 166–169
gift giving, 67
globalization, 96
goals
  vs. activities, 45–46
  of boss, 121–122
  performance, 110–111
Goffman, Erving, 52–53
group dynamics, 32

high-intensity workplaces
  acceptance strategy for, 51–52, 57
  managing, 49–59
  passing strategy for, 52–54, 57
  revealing strategy for, 54–55, 57
high self-monitors, 104, 110
honesty, 118, 130
humor, 88

ideal workers, 49–59
ideas, selling your, 105–106

influence
   horizontal, 68–69
   of managers, 11–12, 13
information
   exclusive, 65, 76
   flow of, between boss and
      subordinates, 118, 129–130
   preferred method for receiving,
      127
integration, of team, 31–32
integrator, 168, 169–170
integrity, 92
interdependencies, 8–9, 13, 29–30
international assignments, 172
introspection, 108

judgment, 23
just-in-time coaching, 44

leaders
   authenticity and, 101–113
   emotional intelligence of, 79–99
   functional, 169
   learning to be, 6
   managers becoming, 165–179
   networking by, 133–149
leadership
   enterprise, 165–179
   styles, 104–105
   team, 19–33
learning, 110–111
learning meetings, 30
left-brain thinking, 178
level shifting, 171
life stories, 112
liking principle, 62–66
limbic system, 86
loss language, 75–76
low self-monitors, 104–105, 106, 110
lunch meetings, 41–42

management responsibilities,
   adjusting to, 1
management time, 151–163
   boss-imposed, 151, 156
   self-imposed, 151–163
   system-imposed, 151, 156
managers
   authority of, 4, 7–12
   becoming leaders, 165–179
   challenges for, 1–6
   as change agents, 14–16
   in high-intensity workplaces,
      49–59
   misconceptions of, 5–17
   power of, 4, 9–12
   smoothly running operations
      and, 14–16
   transitions for new, 1–18
   See also leaders; new managers
maturity, 86
McClelland, David, 85
McGuire, William, 72
meetings
   drop-by, 42
   frequency of, 30
   lunch, 41–42
   with team members, 24
   types of, 30
mental stimulation, 171
mentors/mentoring, 5, 17–18,
   52, 96
mind-set
   for networking, 145–146
   strategic, 170–171
misconceptions, about management, 5–17
mistakes, by new managers, 6, 16
motivation, 81, 82, 84, 92–94
multicultural environments, 111
multifaceted identity, 56–58
mutual dependence, 119–120, 124
mutual expectations, 118, 128–129

negative feedback, 106, 108
neocortex, 86
networking, 106, 133–149
   commitment to, 148–149
   mind-set for, 145–146
   operational, 134, 135–138, 140
   outside-inside connections,
      146–147
   personal, 134, 135, 136, 138–141
   strategic, 134, 135, 136, 140–147
   time for, 147
networks
   contributing to, 147–148
   leveraging your, 137, 145
neurotransmitters, 86
new managers
   challenges for, 1–6, 35–36
   coaching for, 35–36, 44, 142–143
   constructive feedback and, 39,
      46–48
   learning to delegate and, 36–40
   misconceptions of, 5–17
   mistakes by, 6, 16
   projection of confidence by,
      38–39, 42–44
   skill development in, 35–48
   strategic thinking by, 39, 44–46
   support from boss for, 16–18, 38,
      40–42
   transition period for, 1–18
   in unfamiliar role, 104–105
nonwork identity, 56–58, 59

Oncken, Bill, 158–160
operating model, for team, 29–30
operational meetings, 30
operational networking, 134,
   135–138, 140
optimism, 93
organizational change, 14–16, 174
organizational structure, 172–174

outsight, 109
overdependent behavior, 125–126

passing strategy, in high-intensity
   workplaces, 52–54, 57
pattern recognition, 171
peers
   assistance from, 16–18
   relationship building with, 8–9
people skills, 23
performance bar, 93
performance goals, 110–111
performance reviews, 88
personal leadership style, 104–105
personal lives, 49–50, 52,
   57–58, 59
personal narratives, 112
personal networking, 134, 135, 136,
   138–141
persuasion
   authority and, 65, 72–75
   consistency and, 65, 69–72
   ethics and, 77–78
   liking and, 62–66
   natural talent for, 61
   reciprocity and, 64, 66–68
   research on, 72–73
   scarcity and, 65, 75–76
   science of, 61–78
   social proof and, 64, 68–69
playfulness, 108–112
power, of managers, 4, 9–12
praise, 64, 65–66
problem solver, 169, 174, 176
professional development,
   142–143, 173
professional identity, 6, 52

rapport building, 97
reciprocity, 64, 66–68

relationship building, 5, 8-9,
13-14, 18
resource allocation, 67
revealing strategy, in high-intensity
workplaces, 54-55, 57
right-brain thinking, 178
role models, 109-110, 169, 177-178
rookie managers. *See* new managers

sales executives, evaluation of, 175
scarcity, 65, 75-76
self-awareness, 81, 82, 84, 85,
88-89, 123-124
self-confidence, 89
self-image, 112
self-imposed time, 151-163
self-regulation, 81, 82, 84, 89-92
self-understanding, 123-126
similarity, 63-64
social media, 103
social proof, 64, 68-69
social skill, 81, 83, 84, 97-99
Socrates, 73
specialists, 166-169
staff development, 46
status updates, 154
strategic meetings, 30
strategic networking, 134, 135, 136,
140-147
strategic thinking, 39, 44-46,
170-171
strategists, 168, 170-171
subordinate-imposed time, 151-163
subordinates
control of, 4, 12-13
information flow between boss
and, 129-130
managing, 10
mutual dependence between boss
and, 119-120, 124
mutual expectations and, 128-129

overloading, 49
power sharing with, 12-13
relationships with, 5, 8, 13-14,
119-120
transferring initiative to, 161-162
trust building with, 154
wariness of, 10
work styles of, 118, 122-123,
127-128
See also employees
subteams, 29
success
creating conditions for, 15
organizational, 18
superiors
assistance from, 16-18
relationship building with, 8-9,
115-131
See also boss(es)
system-imposed time, 151, 156

tactician, 168, 170-171
team building, 13-14, 20, 30, 36
team culture, 14
team members
assessment of, 24-26
collaboration by, 23-24
expectations for, 22-23
one-on-one meetings with, 24
qualities in, 21, 22-23
replacing underperforming, 26
roles of, 22-23
teams
accelerating development of,
32-33
alignment of, 28-29
assessing, 20-26
composition of, 26-27
empathy and, 95
group dynamics, 32
integration, 31-32

teams (*continued*)
  leading, 19–33
  meetings, 30
  operating model for, 29–30
  reshaping, 26–32
technical competence, 10–11, 36, 81
testimonials, 68–69
Thatcher, Margaret, 108
time
  management, 151–163 (*see also* management time)
  use of boss's, 118, 130–131
time-based rewards, 58–59
training, authenticity, 107
true-to-selfers, 104–105, 106, 110

trust, 154
trustworthiness, 22
Tuckman, Bruce, 20
Tupperware parties, 62–63

unfamiliar roles, 104–105

vision, 81, 178

warrior, 169, 176–177
work hours, 50
work styles, 118, 122–123, 127–128

The most important management ideas all in one place.

We hope you enjoyed this book from *Harvard Business Review*. Now you can get even more with HBR's 10 Must Reads Boxed Set. From books on leadership and strategy to managing yourself and others, this 6-book collection delivers articles on the most essential business topics to help you succeed.

HBR's 10 Must Reads Series

The definitive collection of ideas and best practices on our most sought-after topics from the best minds in business.

- Change Management
- Collaboration
- Communication
- Emotional Intelligence
- Innovation
- Leadership
- Making Smart Decisions

- Managing Across Cultures
- Managing People
- Managing Yourself
- Strategic Marketing
- Strategy
- Teams
- The Essentials

hbr.org/mustreads

Buy for your team, clients, or event.
Visit hbr.org/bulksales for quantity discount rates.